SEPTEMBER

VOLUME 12 / PART 3

Edited by **Grace Emmerson and John Parr**

The Bible Reading Fellowship
OPENING THE BIBLE

Writers in this issue

Romans *The Revd Dr Michael B. Thompson* is Director of Studies at Ridley Hall, Cambridge, and teaches New Testament and Greek for the Cambridge Theological Federation. Originally from the United States, he is an ordained priest in the Episcopal Church. He is the author of *Clothed with Christ*, a study of the influence of Jesus' teachings on Paul's ethics in Romans 12–15.

Ecclesiastes *Mr John Eaton* was formerly Reader in Old Testament studies in the University of Birmingham. His published work includes books on the Psalms and on Job, and most recently *The Circle of Creation: Animals in the Light of the Bible* (illustrated). He has a particular interest in spirituality and the arts.

Matthew 8–20 *The Revd Dr John Parr* is Priest in Charge of Harston and Hauxton near Cambridge, and Director of Continuing Ministerial Education in the Ely Diocese. He is joint-editor of *Guidelines* and editor of BRF's companion to the Gospels and Acts, *Sowers and Reapers*.

Esther *Dr Grace Emmerson* is an honorary lecturer in theology at the University of Birmingham. She has published work on various Old Testament subjects and has lectured to church and other groups on biblical issues. Her involvement in parish work includes time spent in the Diocese of the Arctic. She is joint-editor of *Guidelines* and editor of BRF's companion to the prophetic books of the Old Testament, *Prophets and Poets*.

Psalms *Professor John Rogerson* was Head of the Department of Biblical Studies, University of Sheffield, from 1979 to 1994. He is retiring in 1996 in order to devote his time to writing on theological and ethical issues. An Anglican priest, he has given many lectures to parish and other groups on the study and use of the Bible. He is a former editor of *Guidelines*, and contributed the notes on Jonah and Micah in BRF's companion to the prophetic books of the Old Testament, *Prophets and Poets*.

Christmas and New Year readings *Zoë Bennett Moore* teaches doctrine at Westcott House, Cambridge, and is particularly interested in feminist theology and education. She is married, with three daughters and a stepson.

Editors' Letter

The readings in this issue range over familiar and less familiar parts of the Bible. We shall see quite a contrast between the exuberant expressions of the Christian gospel and the sometimes uncomfortable sentiments found elsewhere. There is an important challenge in holding these two aspects of the biblical message together—nothing less than the call to face squarely some of the cruel realities of life, and to live always in the light of the gospel.

We begin with St Paul's letter to the Romans, which has proved to be one of the most influential Christian writings. A new contributor to *Guidelines*, Michael Thompson is well qualified to lead us through it. By contrast, Ecclesiastes' often gloomy reflections on life remind us of the different perspective that hope of eternal life brings. Our readings in Matthew take us from the beginning of Jesus' healing ministry in Galilee to the threshold of his entry into Jerusalem. Esther is a gripping story of courage in the face of threatened genocide, a horror of all-too-recent memory. John Rogerson, known to our readers over many years, guides us through the pre-Christmas season in meditations on those difficult Psalms which trouble us with their vindictive attitudes. His notes help us to understand them sensitively in the light of Christmas. The Christmas readings by Zoë Bennett-Moore are based on a passage of scripture which is well used at this time of year—the Prologue to St John's Gospel.

Thank you for the steady flow of letters. It's encouraging to know that *Guidelines* continues to stimulate and sometimes provoke you. We wish all our readers much blessing as, with us, they read and ponder the scriptures and share in the true fellowship of prayer.

Grace Emmerson, John Parr
Editors

The BRF Prayer

O God our Father,

in the holy scripture

you have given us your word

to be our teacher and guide:

help us and all the members of our Fellowship

to seek in our reading

the guidance of the Holy Spirit

that we may learn more of you

and of your will for us,

and so grow in likeness to your Son,

Jesus Christ our Lord.

THE BRF
Magazine

Richard Fisher writes. . .

'**F**ifteen per cent of regular churchgoers in England and Wales claim not to have read anything from the Bible *at any time in their lives*.'

These were the shocking findings of a cross-denominational survey commissioned by Bible Society in September 1995.

The sad fact seems to be that more and more churchgoers, who attend church faithfully each Sunday, are neglecting the Bible. They appear to regard it as non-essential to their Christian lives, an old book with nothing to say to them today. How wrong they are! Almost every day we receive letters here at BRF from readers all over the world, telling how a particular Bible passage and comment in *New Daylight* or *Guidelines* has spoken powerfully to them, perhaps challenging, comforting, encouraging them—to the extent that they felt moved to write to tell us.

All of us at BRF have a passion for the Bible, a passion to see others encounter the Bible, to see the Bible come alive for them. We believe the Bible is vital to our on-going Christian lives—that is why we're involved with BRF's ministry.

And we need your help! This is

... consider how you might become involved as a partner in BRF's ministry...

not a plea for financial support, although there's a place for that with regard to the particular projects which BRF supports both in the UK and abroad. Rather, this is an appeal to you, the readers of *Guidelines*, to consider how you might become involved as a partner in BRF's ministry. Could you help us to stimulate Bible reading in your own church and local community? Would you be interested in becoming a BRF Group Secretary or BRF Representative? If you would like to know more about how you could help BRF encourage more people to read the Bible regularly, please let us know. We should be delighted to hear from you.

Sample copies of the notes

Would you like us to send a copy of *Guidelines* or *New Daylight* to a friend or relative, so they can try them for themselves? If so, write to us enclosing an A5 36p s.a.e. (with *their* name and address) and we'll send them a sample copy. Don't forget to let us know which notes to send. Regretfully we can only offer this to readers in the UK.

Of course, if you wish to give someone a year's subscription to the notes, you can do so using the Gift Subscription form on page 157.

New Initiatives

Autumn 1996 sees the launch of two major new initiatives from BRF:

The People's Bible Commentary

A group of major authors have been brought together to create a series of commentaries, which will eventually cover the whole Bible. Written at a popular level, and addressing both the head and the heart, these commentaries are intended for people who want to delve more deeply into the Bible. *The People's Bible Commentaries* are different from any of the commentaries currently available and will be ideal for readers of *Guidelines*, as a complement to the daily notes. See page 16 for a feature article and details of the first volumes.

Livewires

We have some very good news and some sad news. The sad news is that with regret we are discontinuing publication of *First Light*. The current issue will in fact be the last. In recent

Autumn 1996 sees the launch of two major new initiatives from BRF

years the circulation has been declining to a point where we can no longer produce it cost-effectively. We should like to put on record our great thanks to all those who have edited, illustrated and written for *First Light* and its predecessors over the years.

The good news is that *Livewires* will soon be available. Aimed at 8–10 year olds, *Livewires* is a series of Bible-based adventures which will take children on a voyage of discovery into the Bible, its stories and its characters. You can find out more about this exciting new series on page 21.

Don't forget also that each title in BRF's *Lightning Bolts* series offers ten weeks of undated daily Bible readings for 11–14 year olds.

75th Anniversary

January 1997 sees the start of a year of celebration to mark BRF's 75th anniversary—see pages 8–10 for more details of particular events, including a Pilgrimage to the Holy Land.

Special Projects News

There are no major new developments concerning any of the on-going projects which BRF supports. The first one-year volume of daily notes in Romanian is now published, and we hope another will follow in 1997. We will bring you news of any new projects in future issues of the *Magazine*.

Bible Sunday/Bible Reading Promotion Pack

Instead of a specific Bible Sunday Pack, we are this year making available a Bible Reading Promotion Pack, designed for use at any time during the year, including Bible Sunday itself (8 December 1996). The new pack will be available from the end of September, and will be of use to anyone who wants to promote Bible reading, and of course BRF Bible reading resources, within their church. The pack itself will be sent to you free of charge, but we are very grateful for any donations towards its production costs. See page 158 for an order form for the pack.

And so to this issue of *The BRF Magazine* where, in addition to the features already mentioned and the regular columns from Bishop Simon Barrington-Ward and Canon Joy Tetley, you will find a special article 'God Comes First' by Canon John Fenton, and an extract from Bishop Richard Harries' book *A Gallery of Reflections: The Nativity of Christ*. I hope that you will find the *Magazine* informative and of interest, and that you enjoy this issue of the notes.

P.S. We've moved the Gift Subscription and Order Forms to the last pages of the notes to make them easier to tear out and use without damaging your copy.

BRF 75th Anniversary

We first mentioned BRF's forthcoming 75th Anniversary in the January 1996 issue of *The BRF Magazine*. Now at last we can give you an outline of some of the events which will be taking place during the year. Other events are still at the planning stage, and further details will be included in the next issue(s).

Service of Thanksgiving and Rededication

This will take place on Thursday 30 January 1997, in Westminster Abbey, London. It will be an occasion for us to give thanks for 75 years of BRF ministry in many countries around the world, to remember all those who have so faithfully served the Fellowship both on the staff and in the churches over the years, to celebrate all that God is doing in and through BRF today, and to rededicate ourselves for the tasks and challenges that lie ahead.

Bishop Timothy Dudley-Smith has written two new hymns for BRF to mark the occasion of the 75th

Anniversary, and these will be sung for the very first time at the Service.

We hope that many of our readers will be able to join us on this occasion. Admission to the Abbey will be by ticket only—an application form for tickets was included in the May–August issue of the notes.

Group Secretary Days

On certain Saturdays in March, April, June and September here at BRF in Oxford there will be an opportunity for Group Secretaries to come together, to meet members of the BRF team along with some of our authors and contributors to the notes, to see how BRF functions, and to hear more about BRF's ministry, publications and charitable projects. We will be writing to Group Secretaries direct to invite them to join us for one of these days.

'celebrating our fellowship'

Christian Resources Exhibitions

BRF will be at both exhibitions—at Sandown Park, Esher, Surrey in May 1997 and at G-MEX, Manchester in October 1997—and BRF authors will be participating in the lecture programmes. Do come and visit the BRF stand, where you will be able to meet authors and staff, find out more about the work of the Fellowship and see the latest new publications. There will be special offers available on the stand to readers of the notes.

Bible Sunday

We hope that many churches throughout the world will use Bible Sunday (7 December 1997) as a date on which to join us in giving thanks for the Bible itself, and for all those who have worked so tirelessly through the ages to make the scriptures available and accessible to more and more people. An outline service will be available from BRF, which will draw on some of the elements from our own Service of Thanksgiving and Rededication at Westminster Abbey at the beginning of the year. Our churches may be located in different parts of the world, in different time zones, but on that one day, we can all join together, celebrating our fellowship in the scriptures and our partnership in the gospel, with an act of thanksgiving and rededication of ourselves to the task of encouraging others to read the Bible. More details about this service will follow in the next issues of the *Magazine*.

Local events

We hope that many churches and groups will hold their own Bible related events during the year, and link these to BRF's 75th Anniversary. An information pack, with advice and ideas of what you might do in your area, will be available soon—further details to come in the January issue of the *Magazine*.

Pilgrimage to the Holy Land

75th Anniversary Pilgrimage

'**O**nce you have been to the Holy Land you'll never read the Bible in the same way again.' This has been the testimony of countless pilgrims who have visited Israel— and it is certainly the experience of those who have come with BRF. Since 1994 we have taken a group to the Holy Land each year in May. A 75th Anniversary pilgrimage is planned for May 1997 and we hope that you will consider joining us.

Here is an opportunity to visit the land of the Bible itself and to experience something of the places, the geography, the sights, sounds and smells— the hustle and bustle of Jerusalem, the stark beauty of the Judean wilderness, the tranquillity of the Sea of Galilee—all of which will bring the biblical narrative alive in a unique and unforgettable way.

... an opportunity to visit the land of the Bible itself

A panoramic view of Jerusalem from the Mount of Olives; the Garden of Gethsemane; a walking tour of the Old City of Jerusalem; the Via Dolorosa; the Church of the Holy Sepulchre; the Garden Tomb; Bethlehem; Emmaus; Masada; the Dead Sea; Jericho; Nazareth; Cana; the Mount of the Beatitudes; Capernaum; Caesarea Philippi; a cruise on the Sea of Galilee—just some of the highlights of this BRF pilgrimage.

Our itinerary includes seven nights in Jerusalem followed by four in Tiberias on the Sea of Galilee, staying in 4/5 star equivalent hotels. The pilgrimage will be led by BRF's Chief Executive, Richard Fisher.

Comments after previous BRF pilgrimages include: 'a once in a lifetime experience'... 'I don't think life will ever be the same again!'... 'I've been amazed at how my Bible has come alive in a new way as I've read through the Gospels and Acts.'

For an information pack and booking details, please send an A4 25p s.a.e., clearly marked 'Pilgrimage' in the top left hand corner, to the BRF office in Oxford.

Spreading the Word

Many people don't find regular Bible reading and prayer easy. Hand on heart, it's something I have always struggled with. Bible reading notes have certainly helped me over the years and I thank God for those who encouraged me to try them. I also thank God for those who told me not to get a huge guilt complex if I missed a day here and there!

I wonder who encouraged you to start taking *these* notes? Through our subscription surveys, we learned that one person spotted them in hospital when visiting her mother (the man in the next bed had a copy). Another person told us, 'having read *A Feast for Lent*, I felt the need to read my Bible daily.' Many, many people were introduced by friends and relatives and, apart from clergy, these were the two most frequently mentioned factors.

Thank you for the comments you made through these surveys, and also through your letters. We are encouraged by how much you appreciate the notes: 'They have become a daily must...'; 'They are my regular friend..'; 'A life-line...' One person described them as 'an oasis in a parched desert' when she moved away from family and friends.

'I have been a Bible reader for many years,' wrote another reader, 'but am still learning new things with the help of BRF notes.' A lady in her nineties said she appreciated them because she could no longer attend church services or activities. They were helpful to a deaf person because she couldn't follow the sermons in church, or on TV.

Spending time with God through regular Bible reading and prayer is an important discipline—a discipline which is also a delight. Many people in our churches haven't discovered this yet. So, if BRF notes and resources help you, why not introduce someone you know to them? Show them your copy or think

> *Many, many people were introduced by friends and relatives*

about giving them as a gift, perhaps through our Gift Subscription scheme. They are a gift that can be enjoyed every day of the year. Don't forget that there is a large print version of *New Daylight*. And there are audio cassettes for those who are visually impaired and registered blind.

Many of our current readers began taking BRF notes as children or young people, and the regular habit has stayed with them over the years. With the exciting new *Livewires* notes for young readers, and *Lightning Bolts* for teenagers, we can help the next generation to develop the habit too. I know that some of you parents and grandpar-

'They are part of my prayer life, and I feel part of a very special community.'

ents are already doing just that. BRF notes make a very good present for godparents to give, and they are ideal for confirmation at all ages.

One person has commented: 'They are part of my prayer life, and I feel part of a very special community.' That is exactly what we want. We hope that you feel part of that special community, *The Bible Reading Fellowship*, as well. During the coming anniversary year, please will you spread the word, and help us to enlarge that community of those who draw near to God through regular Bible reading and prayer.

Jackie Vincent

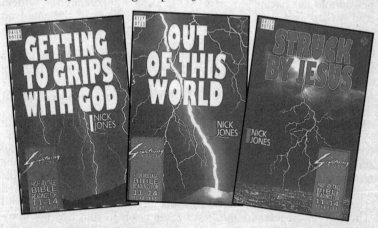

Lightning Bolts daily notes are available from your local Christian bookshop or, in case of difficulty, direct from BRF. See order form, page 159.

The Vision of God: part 2

Joy Tetley

We search for a God who constantly searches for us. Such, indeed, is the witness of the scriptures. They point us to a many-splendoured and multi-faceted vision; one that opens windows rather than closes doors.

The scriptures disclose a tantalizing God. A God who will not be tamed or confined. A God who breaks out of boundaries, even sacred boundaries. A God who constantly surprises and challenges, yet is utterly trustworthy and faithful. A God whose burning holiness takes him into the middle of what we call the 'real world'. A God whose passionate love puts him on the receiving end of savage abuse. A God bursting with creativity, vitality and joy, who nonetheless weeps with those who weep. A God who is greater than all that is, yet with a personal touch that is awesome in its intensity.

This God yearns for communion with humankind, calling forth a responsive longing.

In these ancient documents from a faraway world, we can still come face to face with ourselves and with the living God.

The scriptures were born out of experience; out of faith and doubt; out of celebration and struggle; out of joy and anguish. In many and various ways, they seek to put into words the impact of God. They are prompted by particular, often compelling, situations. They are coloured in their expression by their culture, religious background and context.

But they are nonetheless recognizable. All human life is there. And all human life in all shades of relationship with a God who both comforts and confronts. In these ancient documents from a faraway world, we can still come face to face with ourselves and with the living God.

Today both the Church and the world are full of questions; curious questions, sharp questions, heartbreaking questions, inarticulate questions. So are the scriptures. Too often the Bible is thought of as a neatly tied-up package of propositions, a rule book with dollops of human interest to help us swallow the medicine. What a travesty! What an opportunity lost—a chance to get to grips and to wrestle with the living God.

When we allow the unpredictable Spirit of truth to take hold of the scriptures, they are anything but cut and dried. Like the God we meet in them, they are living and active. They refuse to be domesticated.

The Bible contains all sorts of different writings. Throughout all of them there is a dialogue going on. A dialogue between God and humanity, humanity and God. A dialogue characterized by passion on both sides. Strong feelings abound, whether of joy and delight or of hurt and anger. The conversation is rarely a superficial one, though it can be very mundane in form. Sometimes it is far from polite.

Yet of such a tempestuous exchange is rich relationship born. And the scriptures are fundamentally about relationship, even when dealing with matters of law, as Psalm 119 so eloquently testifies.

The dialogue goes on. It *must* go on if there is to be any hope of deepening understanding. Questions are near to the heart of the matter. As you engage with the scriptures, notice what a significant role questions play in the divine/human dialogue. They crop up all over the place.

God's most important question of all comes to us in the form of Jesus. As someone once put it, Jesus is an arresting combination of question mark and exclamation mark. In Jesus, God exclaims both in joy and in pain, both in tenderness and in anger, 'I love you'. In Jesus, God asks, without any coercion, 'Can you love *me*?' In their various ways, all of the Gospel traditions confront us with that searching invitation.

And all of the Gospels present Jesus as posing a good few questions. From the records we have, it seems fairly clear that Jesus made people think, that he was economical with straight answers, that he made people confused and angry, that he aroused hatred and conspiracy as well as wonder and devotion.

In Jesus, God exclaims both in joy and in pain, both in tenderness and in anger, 'I love you'.

'Who then is this?' That question remains with us. It is our duty and our joy to engage with it, struggle with it, work at it—at every level of our being. Not just for our own sakes, but for God's sake, and for the sake of God's world.

The questioning God, incarnate in Jesus, does, of course, respect our freedom. We can ignore the questions. Or, like the scriptural people of God, we can hazard a whole variety of answers.

Like our forebears, too, we have the freedom to throw our questions at God. The Bible leaves us in no doubt that it's a two-way process. Much of the biblical witness seems to suggest that we are positively encouraged to question God. It's an important part of maturing relationship.

According to scripture, honesty really is the best policy. That is powerfully demonstrated in the cry of desolation from the cross, recorded in Mark's Gospel: 'My God, my God, why hast thou forsaken me?'

Why? That question is always with us. It comes from the heart of human experience. It gives us the most profound hope that, somehow, God feels the force of that

Much of the biblical witness seems to suggest that we are positively encouraged to question God. It's an important part of maturing relationship.

question; that, somehow, God knows what it's like to feel God-forsaken.

And out of that great, unanswered question, shouted into the darkness, comes a new beginning—not an answer but a response, a way through that breaks the bounds of possibility. There, quite literally, is the crux of the matter. The God we encounter in the Bible is, at heart, God of cross and resurrection: the God who comes to us where we are and goes to hell and back with us and for us.

To this God we can respond. To this God we can entrust our lives. With this God we can participate in the adventure of redemption. With this God we can reach out in love to the world.

To be continued

Joy Tetley *is Principal of the East Anglican Ministerial Training Course and specializes in the areas of ministry and biblical studies. She is author of* Sunday by Sunday—*commentaries and prayers for the Sundays of the Church's year (available from your local Christian bookshop or, in case of difficulty, direct from BRF, see order form, page 159).*

The People's Bible Commentary series

A utumn 1996 sees the start of something new from BRF. We are publishing a brand new series of devotional commentaries which will eventually cover every book of the Bible.

Many people would like to read and to study the whole Bible—but they would also like a guide to help them. *The People's Bible Commentary* will provide just the guidance and the help they are looking for. Each book of the Bible is divided into a number of passages and for each passage there is a double page spread of commentary and a prayer. Thus you can work systematically through a whole book in manageable sections. And of course this approach is ideal for daily use if you wish.

The People's Bible Commentary aims to do two things:

To instruct the head—so that the reader's understanding of the text is enlarged.

To warm the heart—so that people find themselves worshipping and praying in response to what they read.

Six or seven volumes will be published each year for the next seven years, so that people will be able to build up a complete library. If they use the books as intended they will find themselves not only with a much broader and deeper understanding and appreciation of the Bible itself—with its variety and richness—but also they will find their own faith and relationship with God to have been immeasurably enriched.

Who is the series for?

These day-by-day commentaries will take a reverent approach to scripture: neither dogmatic nor dismissive. They will be useful to people who would like to study the Bible in a serious but not academic way, and also to people who teach or preach the scriptures. They would make a marvellous gift for a children's or youth leader, lay reader or minister.

The Bible is valued by every Christian tradition, telling the sacred story of the faith which all Christian people share. The Vatican II Documents speak of the 'rich and rewarding consequences of constant Bible reading, not only by the clergy but also by the laity'. This book, the Bible, which we all share can make us far more aware of the things which we have in common, rather than the things which divide us. The editors and writers of *The People's Bible Commentary* have deliberately been chosen from different traditions.

There are three General Editors, all of whom contribute regularly to *New Daylight*:

The Revd Shelagh Brown—writer, commissioning editor for BRF and Editor of *New Daylight*.

The Revd Dom Henry Wansbrough, OSB—Editor of The New Jerusalem Bible, Master of St Benet's Hall in Oxford, lecturer and broadcaster.

The Revd Canon David Winter—former head of religious broadcasting at the BBC, writer and broadcaster.

Who are the writers?

The writers are either biblical scholars or parish priests and all are skilled communicators. The first seven volumes will be:

1. **Genesis**, by The Revd Henry Wansbrough, who is also a General Editor of the series.

2. **Job**, by The Revd Canon David Atkinson, who is Canon Missioner of Southwark Cathedral, London, and the author of *Job* in The Bible Speaks Today series (IVP).

3. The first six of what are known as The Minor Prophets or **The Book of the Twelve**. This volume, by The Revd Canon Joy Tetley, will contain Hosea, Joel, Amos, Obadiah, Jonah and Micah. Joy Tetley is Principal of the East Anglian Ministerial Training Course, a writer, a regular contributor to *The Church Times*, and author of *Sunday by Sunday*.

4. **Mark**, by The Revd R.T. France. Formerly Principal of Wycliffe Theological College Oxford, and author of major works on Mark, Luke and the ending of John, Dick France is now Rector of a group of churches in the Diocese of Hereford.

5. **1 Corinthians**, by Professor Jerome Murphy-O'Connor, OP, of Ecole Biblique in Jerusalem. He has taught in the Ecole Bibloque for many years, and is the acknowledged expert on Paul's Corinthian correspondence and the intertestamental literature.

6. **Galatians**, by The Revd Canon John Fenton. Formerly Principal of St Chad's College, Durham and a Canon of Christ Church in Oxford, John Fenton is the author of many books, including *Finding the Way Through John*, *Finding the Way through Mark* (Mowbrays 1995) and *The Matthew Passion*, BRF's Lent book for 1996.

7. **Revelation**, by The Revd Marcus Maxwell, who is Vicar of Heaton Mersey in Lancashire, England, and a regular contributor to *New Daylight*.

At the time of going to press with *The BRF Magazine* prices for the first volumes in *The People's Bible Commentary* are still to be finalized. Please ask at your local bookshop or contact BRF direct for more details.

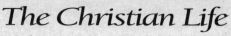

The Christian Life

Simon Barrington-Ward

Root and Branches: The Vision Symbol

There were four of us at the beginning praying together in the Coventry Diocesan Retreat House. We had been asked to go away and devise a vision statement for the diocese which would embody all the aspirations which we had sensed in our travels round the diocese.

The Giving of the Symbol

There had been a number of initiatives from the centre already which asked all the parishes for responses, such as 'Deanery Congresses' and a 'Call to Mission'. We had been told that people did not want to take part in another long, drawn-out process.

They wanted the Bishop to come out with something which would speak to every parish. He could then go round and, by listening and looking, help people to see how the things for which they were struggling in their life and worship were both challenged and fulfilled by the vision he presented. Thus it would draw the whole diocese together into one movement of the Spirit.

> *They wanted the Bishop to come out with something which would speak to every parish.*

We ourselves, the two bishops and two archdeacons, struggled for a day to draw out all the trends and needs we had observed. By nightfall we were clear that what was wanted was not a great screed but rather a symbol, something with perhaps a *few* words on it which could be filled out in varying ways in different settings.

We were also clear that it must all spring out of a movement of receptive prayer, prayer that essentially consisted of *our* being grasped by God's grace and truth in Christ.

Two years earlier, in the very room in which we were now sitting, some visitors from India, East Germany, South Africa and China (the elderly Bishop Stephen Wang and his wife, Jing An, and a younger priest) and from other places, had said to us, 'in your church here you have too many vines! Your greatest need is to return and seek to abide in the one vine, and all to be branches in that one vine.' As we sat there I could still see their faces in my mind's eye.

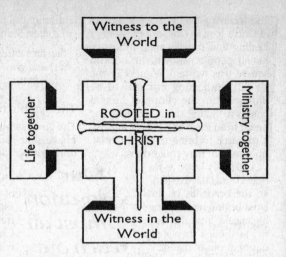

Next morning, coming down early, I saw that one of the others had already broken beyond all our scribbled shapes of the night before and set there the Mercian Cross, the symbol of our own and other dioceses in this area, a cross that goes back perhaps to St Chad, who founded our churches.

It has a square in the centre covering the meeting point between the cross beam and the vertical, and squares to the left and the right, the top and the bottom, at the ends of each beam of the cross. At first it seemed too heavy and static to me, but, as we worked with it, gradually the dynamic and the movement and the integrity of it came home to me.

The Symbol takes shape

At the centre we wrote the words 'Rooted in Christ' to stand for the prayerful experience of God's love, tender and yet sharp. His 'severe mercy' enfolding us in Christ, through the Spirit. At either end of the crossbar: to the left, 'Life Together' to convey a breaking and remaking of relationships, found in the cross of Christ, drawing us into a deeper unity with each other; to the right, 'Ministry Together'. That is a release of confidence and of gifts mutually exercised, which the Spirit flowing out from the brokenness of the cross could give to us.

In the square above were the words, 'Witness *to* the World', speaking of that which we had primarily to bring to others around us, albeit quite largely through listening

19

and receiving first, of the good news of God's love in Christ, a message, a healing and transforming influence for all people. And in the bottom square was written 'Witness in the World', indicating our call to be plunged into the efforts of human beings to change the world, learning much from them and yet having also a resource to bring them in Christ, upon whom they could draw.

Gradually I saw, as we prayed and talked together, the branches of the cross beginning to spring organically from the centre, as though they grew out of it, out of that genuine root of prayer and worship, of receiving Christ's forgiveness and yielding oneself to his Lordship, repentant and yet deeply accepted and released, 'confident in self-despair'.

All that we seek to be or to do must rise up out of this root. Ephesians 3:14 'rooted and grounded in love' came to mind, out from which flows the power to grasp, 'with all the saints' more of the breadth and length and height and depth.

Our exploration, as a diocese and as a Church, of all the far reaching implications of God's great love for us, must all reach out from this central and constantly sustained encounter with his living presence in and amongst us. This was a Celtic cross after all, and we could sense how

'the tormented wood will cure its hurt and grow into a tree... the Tree of Life for us all.'

The Symbol takes over

The good symbol takes over, and as I have gone round the diocese with it, that is how it seems to have happened. We dreamt of obeying the injunction of our saintly visitors, especially our dear old frail but indomitable Chinese bishop and his wife, people who had passed through all the horrors of the Cultural Revolution and had suffered much, people who saw deeply into us but with the most affirming and encouraging gaze, urging us to start with a new and deeper 'abiding'.

We look for a movement of prayer across the diocese and a deeper experience of the fulness of God's judgment and mercy and love for each and for all.

Our exploration ...must all reach out from this central and constantly sustained encounter with his living presence in and amongst us.

Simon Barrington-Ward is Bishop of Coventry and author of the BRF book *The Jesus Prayer*. Available from your local Christian bookshop or see order form, page 159.

Focus Spot: Livewires

Parents, grandparents and friendly adults: please show this letter to any children who you think would be interested in *Livewires*.

 Hi! We're just dropping by to tell you about an exciting new adventure that's coming your way.

BRF are launching a new series for 8-10 year olds called *Livewires* and they've asked us to be in it! We said 'yes!', of course - so here we are, the Livewire kids. We can't wait to introduce ourselves and to invite you to join us on the adventure.

This is us in Annie-log's bedroom - that's Annie-log sitting with Boot (he's her computer). Boot's very quiet at the moment, but when Annie-log types a Bible verse on his keyboard, he starts making a whirring sound and, before we know it, we all get whooshed into his disc drive. Boot says we're going 'on-line'. Tychi - he's Boot's mouse - has to hold on very tight when it happens. Boot comes with us into the Bible and grows hands and feet - complete with roller blades - so he can whizz around with us. He really makes us laugh because he looks so comical with his keyboard tucked under his arm - Boot says he can't see the funny side of it. He often gives us helpful hints when we get stuck and directs us if we get a bit lost.

Annie-log's got a younger sister called Data - that's her sitting on the bed. Half the time we wonder if she's on another planet, then she comes out with something really intelligent, or finds something we've all been searching for for ages. She's full of surprises.

Digit - that's him with the shades, sitting on the top bunk - and Quartz are twins. They're in the same class

as Annie-log at school. Feel sorry for their poor teacher.

Then there's Tim. Must be time for the annual haircut soon. It's a good job his dog, Tempo, can see clearly. Tempo's a great sport - he doesn't say a lot, but we know what he's thinking. And last of all there's Little Ben. He's the youngest. We're all great friends and are looking forward to having lots of fun exploring the Bible with you.

Our first two books are coming out in November. So get on down to your local Christian bookshop - or you can order them direct from BRF if you want to.

In *Footsteps and Fingerprints* you can find out how our adventures began one winter's night while we were playing on Annie-log's computer. Amazing things started to happen when we typed Bible verses on Boot's keyboard - before we knew it he'd started whirring and whooshing - and there we were, going on-line... you'll never guess where we landed. Let's just say that if you've ever jumped feet first into a muddy puddle you'll know how we felt.

Then in *Families and Feelings* Boot landed us at the top of a tree... we couldn't imagine *where* we were, until we met someone sitting by a well - what a story he had to tell. Why not join us on our adventure and find out what happened next?

Boot says you'll meet lots of different people when you come on adventures with us. In fact, there's not many people in the Bible you *won't* meet. There are eighteen volumes in the *Livewires* series and every single one of them is packed with things to do, things to find out and things to think about. Then there's a diary page for you to fill in with your own special thoughts. Top secret stuff! The good thing is, the books aren't dated, so you can start reading them when-ever you like. If you want to you can read a bit more of our adventure each day - or you can just pick up with us when you feel like it. We don't mind either way.

Anyway, better go now... Annie-log is about to type something on Boot's keyboard - we can't wait to find out what it is.

See you in November. Bye...

The Livewires

The Livewires

p.s. At the time of going to press with *The BRF Magazine* prices for *Livewires* are still to be finalized. Please ask at your local Christian bookshop or contact BRF direct for more details.

A Gallery of Reflections: The Nativity of Christ

An extract from the BRF book by Richard Harries

Lettering of the beginning of Chapter 2, St Matthew's Gospel by Eric Gill

(The typography, engraving and design form part of The Four Gospels, produced by the Golden Cockerell Press in 1931.)

From at least the fifth century, Christians began to decorate scriptural texts with small illustrations. In due course the custom grew up of turning the initial letter of a book or chapter into a picture. There are many gorgeous initial letters in the illuminated manuscripts of the Middle Ages.

Eric Gill (1882–1940) helped to revive this craft. He began by earning his living as a letter-cutter but became well-known as a sculptor, engraver and writer—as well as a typographer. In 1913 he became a Roman Catholic and was commissioned to make the *Stations of the Cross* at Westminster Cathedral which, together with his *Prospero and Ariel* on the outside of Broadcasting House in London, are his best-known sculptures. He founded a religious guild of craftsmen with the object of promoting a revival of a religious attitude to art and craftsmanship.

All Gill's work, like this lettering and illustration, is characterized by clear, bold outlines and linear elegance. Here our eyes are drawn to the three kings with their hands upraised and we follow their figures down the flowing lines of their bodies and the folds of their garments. They are not kneeling but, as it were, saying, 'Hail, king of the Jews.' They could be figures from a ballet.

Mary, similarly, is in a graceful posture as she kneels, whilst the Christ child is presented naked and unashamed. He is held forth without covering or adornment for all to see. The great diagonal of the 'N' across the picture seems to give added emphasis to the 'NOW' of the birth of Jesus.

There seem to be no hidden depths in this illustration. All is expressed in the line and the movement; all, we might say, is incarnate—made flesh in what is visible and tangible.

The letters are of a piece with the picture in their boldness, style and elegance; letters and illustration form a unity.

Gill brought before the Christ child all the grace and elegance and style of which he was capable. There is a balletic beauty in the gestures and movement. It is a refreshing contrast to the hurried, scruffy, graceless way in which we live so much of our lives. If we are capable of any grace of body or mind, elegance of movement or life, beauty of design or art, this too is a gift worthy to bring and which is graciously received.

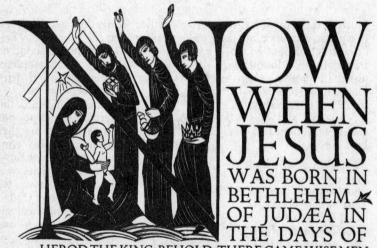

NOW WHEN JESUS WAS BORN IN BETHLEHEM OF JUDÆA IN THE DAYS OF HEROD THE KING, BEHOLD, THERE CAME WISE MEN FROM THE EAST TO JERUSALEM, SAYING, WHERE IS he that is born King of the Jews? for we have seen his star in the east, & are come to worship him.

A Gallery of Reflections: the Nativity of Christ is available from your local Christian bookshop or, in case of difficulty, direct from BRF (see order form, page 159).

God Comes First

John Fenton

On 8 June 1941 I had the good fortune to be in St Mary's Church in Oxford and to hear C.S. Lewis preach a sermon on 'The Weight of Glory'. It was published soon after in *Theology* (volume XLIII, pages 263ff) and can now be found in a collection of his talks, *Screwtape Proposes a Toast* (Fount Paperbacks, 1977).

Much of the sermon has remained in my head ever since, but there was one particular passage that I have frequently found myself quoting. I looked it up recently to see if I had remembered it correctly and was glad to find that I had. Lewis says:

> 'I read in a periodical the other day that the fundamental thing is how we think of God. By God Himself, it is not! How God thinks of us is not only more important, but infinitely more important.'

Put that way, it is obviously true: our eternal state depends entirely on God; in any case, what we think about him is bound to be partial, fragmentary, needing correction and in itself totally inadequate; whereas, by definition what he thinks about us must be complete, exhaustive and irreversible.

Before I heard the sermon, I had not put these points together or noticed this contrast between them. I had realised that it was important how we thought about God. I was studying theology, so knew that it was largely a history of quarrels about how to say the least unworthy things about him who cannot be described; but I had not seen how this is of very little importance compared with God's attitude to us. I should have done. There was so much in

'I read. . . that the fund-amental thing is how we think of God. By God Himself, it is not!'

St Paul's letters where he contrasted our relationship with God with his relationship with us. For example:

> *While we were still helpless, Christ died for the wicked...*

> *Christ died for us while we were yet sinners...*

> *When we were God's enemies, we were reconciled to him through the death of his Son.*

> *Romans 5:6–11*

There was also the passage in Galatians when Paul corrected what he had just written (whether deliberately or inadvertantly, I do not know). He was, presumably, dictating the letter to his scribe; what he had said was:

> *Now that you do acknowledge God...*

what he changed it to was:

> *Now that he has acknowledged you*

> *Galatians 4:9*

This is exactly Lewis's point: our acknowledgement of God follows from God's acknowledgement of us and depends upon it. We did not find him: he found us.

God loved us before we loved, or could love him. God's love of us rendered possible and actual our love of God.

Twenty years before Lewis preached this sermon, a great Roman Catholic lay theologian, Friedrich von Hügel, had made the same point in an address that he delivered in 1921:

> *God not only loves us more and better than we can ever love ourselves;... but God loved us before we loved, or could love Him. God's love of us rendered possible and actual our love of God.*

He went on to refer to St Bernard, who

> *Bids his monks rise never so early for their night choir prayer in coldest mid-winter; they will find God awake, Him the awakener; they will find Him waiting for them, always anticipating even their earliest watches.*

> *Essays and Addresses: second series, 1926, pages 224f.*

This way of seeing things is known as the doctrine of the prevenience of God; that is, that he comes first, before us, and makes our lives and actions possible. If we believed this, it would affect the way in which we saw our relationships with those with whom we did not agree; particularly with those with whom we did not agree on religious or ethical questions.

Any group of people formed to do a job—to preserve old buildings, for example, or to oppose fox-hunting, or to work for justice—can only survive as a group if there is broad agreement among its members on the aims and methods to be pursued. When there is no such agreement, the group is forced to divide, and some must leave it.

It would be a mistake to think of Christianity in this way. Christians are not a group of people who have come together to forward the teaching of Jesus or to establish the Kingdom of God or to do any other such thing. They do not see themselves as having cho-sen Christ: he, they believe, has chosen them (John 15:16). It is not appropriate for any of them to judge somebody else's domestic servant (Romans 14:4; Matthew 7:1).

There can be vast differences between the way that one follower of Christ sees the truth, and the way another sees it.

There can be vast differences between the way that one follower of Christ sees the truth, and the way another sees it. What matters is that both of them believe that God has prevented (come in advance of) their thoughts and insights; that these are partial and inadequate; and that how God thinks of us is infinitely more important. That is enough to hold us together, in spite of our differences.

John Fenton *was formerly Principal of St Chad's College, Durham and a Canon of Christ Church in Oxford. He is the author of* The Matthew Passion, *published by BRF, which is available from your local Christian bookshop or, in case of difficulty, direct from BRF. See order form, page 159.*

Use your PC for Bible reading

Day by Day for Windows

BRF's first electronic publication is another first—the first Windows-based daily Bible reading notes published in the UK.

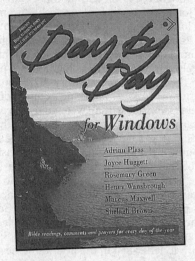

If you have an IBM compatible PC (386 processor or higher) running Windows 3.1 or above then you can use your computer's capabilities to help your daily Bible reading.

When you run *Day by Day for Windows*, you are presented with a one-sentence 'thought for the day' displayed against one of a variety of seasonal scenes. You can then follow up the daily thought by reading the Bible text for the day with a reflection on it from one of a number of authors including Adrian Plass and Joyce Huggett. All were previously published in book form in *Day by Day* volume 1.

The program allows you to search the notes by a number of keywords, and by Bible reference. It also keeps you in touch with the Church calendar, and major feast days. *Day by Day for Windows* provides a year's worth of daily Bible readings. Regular upgrades provide a further year's material.

Available from your local Christian bookshop or, in case of difficulty, direct from BRF. See order form, page 159.

The Letter to the Romans

When Paul dictated this letter from a seaport at Corinth sometime in the winter of AD55/56 or 56/57, he had been a Christian for scarcely more than two decades. Little did he know that his words would continue to ignite, inform and motivate Christian faith for two millennia. John Chrysostom of Antioch, the most famous preacher in the fourth century, had Romans read to him twice a week. Reading Romans 13:13–14 transformed Augustine's life. Martin Luther found God's grace in Romans 1:17. John Wesley felt his heart 'strangely warmed' when reading Luther's preface to his commentary on the letter. In this century, Karl Barth's study of Romans was a trumpet blast reawakening a slumbering Church.

Paul's original reasons for writing were quite practical. Because he hoped to preach as far west as Spain, he sought the support of the Roman Christians as a *missionary* base (15:18–24, 28). Being 'sent on' his journey (15:24) would include provision of food, money, means of transport, letters of introduction and perhaps escort along the way. To that end, Paul needed to produce an *introductory* letter, since he had never visited Rome. His gospel (good news) of grace in Christ and freedom for Gentiles (non-Jews) from the (Old Testament) Law had led some to misunderstand and distort Paul's ideas (see e.g. 3:8; 6:1). As he prepared to return to Jerusalem in the near future he anticipated a hostile reaction from his more conservative Jewish kinsmen (15:25, 30f.). Paul wanted to ensure that the Roman believers would understand his teaching and pray for him (15:30–31).

Another reason for writing is disputed, but many see a *pastoral* purpose in the letter. From his friends in Rome (ch. 16), Paul knew that the congregations there differed among themselves. There were particular tensions between the 'weak' and the 'strong' believers (ch. 14–15). As we shall see, chapters 12–16 reflect Paul's concern to unite Jewish and Gentile Christians in Rome, not only to give him a solid base of support, but also because of his long-standing concern for the Romans themselves (15:15f., 23; cf. 1:8–15). The issue of the relationship of Jews and Gentiles in God's plan dominates the letter (cf. 1:16), as seen for example in the questions 'Who is a Jew?' in 2:25–29 and 'Who are the elect of God?' (1:7; 8:33; 9:6–13; 11:5–7, 28–32), and in the hope that both Jew and Gentile can praise God together (15:8–12). Therefore, although Romans has a timeless quality and is as close to a 'systematic theology' of Paul as we can find among his letters, like his other writings it addressed a particular historical situation.

2–8 SEPTEMBER   ROMANS 1:1—4:25

1 An introduction and the theme *Read Romans 1:1–17*

In the first seventeen verses Paul does three things. First, he says 'hello', in the process briefly introducing himself, his mission and his message (vv. 1–7). Secondly, he tells the Romans how he feels about visiting them (vv. 8–15). His attitude is one of thanksgiving, prayer and longing that he might visit them and share his message. Finally, he states in a nutshell the theme of his letter (vv. 16–17). The key words here are 'power', 'faith', and 'righteousness'.

Although similar in form, the salutations at the beginning of Paul's letters often offer important clues about what was uppermost in the apostle's mind. His gospel did not spring from his own imaginings, but was promised beforehand by God's prophets in scripture (v. 2; see 3:21). The wording of 1:3f. is likewise very Jewish, including some unusual language (for Paul) and reminding his readers of his gospel's Jewish roots—an important signal to Gentile Christians who were sometimes tempted to ridicule their Jewish fellow believers (11:13–19; ch. 14). The focus of Paul's gospel is Christ, the Davidic Messiah fully shown to be God's Son with power by the resurrection (v. 4). Through Christ, Paul has been empowered to call all people (including the Romans) to an obedience of faith. For Paul, the faith that counts is a trusting in the person of Jesus Christ.

After the opening salutation in his letters, Paul usually finds something to thank God about and to pray for his hearers; in the case of the Romans he is thankful for their faith, and prayerful to visit them. We can see the humanness of Paul when, after expressing his strong desire to come and strengthen them with his message, he catches himself and acknowledges that the giving will not be one-sided—he has something to learn from them too (vv. 11–12).

Paul's theme (vv. 16–17) is that the gospel is the means through which God's righteousness is being revealed to all who believe. Elsewhere 'righteousness' can refer to God's justice, the uprightness he demands of us, or a right status with him, but here Paul is most likely speaking of God's faithful character and saving power. God revealed himself first and most clearly to his chosen people, but now membership in his family is no longer a matter of descent—Gentiles as well as Jews can have a right relationship with him through faith.

2   No excuse for the Gentiles *Read Romans 1:18–32*

Although Paul's message is essentially good news, a gospel of *salvation* begs the question of 'deliverance from what?' So he begins to make his case that humanity as a whole stands in need. He focuses first on the Gentiles (vv. 18–32), and then on the Jews (2:1—3:8), before concluding that both groups are alienated from God (3:9–20).

Using traditional language echoing the temptation in the garden of Eden (Genesis 3), the golden calf incident (Exodus 32; Psalm 106:19f.) and Wisdom 12–15, Paul is not trying to prove God's existence, but to indict humanity for failing to maintain a right relationship with the Creator. Despite knowing from the evidence of nature that God exists, people have turned away from him and have come under his wrath, becoming subject to futility and worshipping idols (vv. 18–23). The outcome of this, says Paul, is not enlightenment, but spiritual darkness and a distorted perspective.

Our alienation has its roots in a refusal to honour (literally, 'to glorify') God or to thank him (v. 21). Impurity (vv. 24f.), unnatural passions (vv. 26f.) and all sorts of destructive behaviour (vv. 28–32) result from turning from the Creator to the creation. A frustrated relationship with God leads to frustrated relationships with others.

Two issues deserve special attention. First, by God's 'wrath' Paul does not mean an irrational outburst or unreasonable emotion, but God's holy and just response to sin. In this passage, God's wrath appears in his allowing us to proceed on our chosen path, so that we reap what we sow. It is important to remember that Paul will eventually go on to show that God has not ultimately left us alone, but has intervened to draw us back to himself in Christ.

Second, Paul is not singling out homosexuality as something worse than any of the other activities listed afterwards (vv. 28–32); he cites it here because in Jewish tradition homosexuality was widely regarded as something contrary to the created order and therefore indicative of a skewed perspective. Paul does not say that homosexual relations bring God's wrath, but rather that they are an evidence of it—a sign that our relationships are flawed.

3   No excuse for the religious *Read Romans 2:1–16*

Up until this point, Jewish hearers of the letter would have added their 'Amen' to Paul's indictment of (what they would recognize as) *Gentile* failure to acknowledge and worship God. Now, however, Paul unexpectedly turns the tables on those who feel superior. Beginning in 2:1 and continuing until 3:20 he argues that the failure of religious Jews as well as Gentiles to live up to God's standard shows the universal need for restoration of a right relationship with God.

Again echoing Jewish tradition, Paul asserts that God will impartially judge all people on the basis of what they do (vv. 1–11; see Psalm 62:12; Proverbs 24:12). Like Jesus who warned against setting ourselves up as judges (Matthew 7:1f.) and like James who wrote that faith without works is dead (James 2:26), he stresses the danger of spiritual pride that fails to practise what it preaches. All will have to give an account on the day of judgment. God's impartial justice ensures that Jewish behaviour will reap the same penalty or reward as that of the Gentiles.

Some think that the judgment with a positive outcome (vv. 7, 10) must be hypothetical, because otherwise it would contradict Paul's overall argument of salvation by faith rather than works. This however assumes a false dichotomy of faith and obedience, and distorts the apostle's teaching. For Paul, faith is not something that merely exists in the mind or heart. It works through love (Galatians 5:6) and bears fruit that is recognizable (Galatians 5:22f.).

33

Continuing to build his case, Paul asserts that possession of the (Old Testament) Law is no safeguard to judgment (vv. 12–16). Again, like James he reminds his readers that it is not the hearers but the doers of the Law that are right with God (vv. 13; cf. James 1:22–25). Paul implies that there are Gentiles who do a better job at obedience than some Jews, because they have obeyed what light they have been given apart from the Law. Paul is not however addressing the issue of the fate of unevangelized Gentiles as a subject in itself; he draws in the Gentiles here in order to puncture Jewish attitudes of superiority and boasting.

4 A painful conclusion? *Read Romans 2:17—3:20*

The biggest crisis in the early Church was not about finances, morality or leadership, but about something that is no longer an issue for us: did Gentiles have to become Jews first in order to be part of God's family? Did they *need* to keep the Law—specifically, get themselves circumcised if male, maintain the dietary laws, and observe the sabbath and other holy days? Paul had been attacked throughout his ministry for teaching that they did not, but the first Christians were Jews, most of whom continued to observe their ancient customs. Many felt that Paul's teaching undermined God's faithfulness and righteousness. If God gave the old covenant and the Law to his chosen people, how could he still be just, if the Law is no longer a requirement for the chosen people of the new covenant? Isn't God being inconsistent? How can he be trusted? Paul wants to show that even with the benefit of the Law, the Jews also fall short and need the new relationship that comes with Christ, apart from that Law.

Explicitly addressing the Jews, Paul points out that divinely given privileges do not ensure God's acceptance of them (2:17–29). Their supposed superiority had not led them to better conduct overall (2:17–24). Some find in Paul's sharp language here echoes of Jesus' warnings to the Pharisees (Matthew 23); perhaps we hear reflection on Paul's own past as a Pharisee who zealously persecuted the Christians. More radical is his claim that physical circumcision is no guarantee of ultimately belonging to God's people (2:25–29). Circumcision's value to Judaism in Paul's day was immense: thousands of Jews had died to preserve this custom during the Maccabean revolt in the second century BC.

Paul anticipates that his charges raise big questions. He states the questions and starts to answer them in 3:1–8, but decides to postpone full answers until chapters 6–11. Returning to his main point in 3:9, he begins to wind up his case with a collection of quotations from the Psalms. They form a testimony summarizing humanity's distance from God, and for Paul their inclusion in the Law shows that they speak to the Jews as well as to Gentiles (2:19). Paul's conclusion is a painful one that he must have stated often: the Law brings a knowledge of sin and failure, but it cannot make us right with God (3:20).

5 Acceptance is a gift *Read Romans 3:21–31*

This passage is a theological lodestone, offering Paul's understanding of the significance of Jesus in a highly concentrated form. Crucial new words here include 'grace' (v. 24, unmerited favour or kindness to us in spite of our failures), 'redemption' (v. 24, deliverance from bondage at a cost), and 'expiation' (removal of sin) or 'propitiation' (appeasement of wrath) in 3:25, although more modern translations simplify with the phrase 'sacrifice of atonement'. 'Atonement' speaks of our being put *at one* with God.

The most important words however are the first two: 'But now'. With the coming of Christ, the situation changed for ever. No longer is it necessary to become a Jew first and keep the Law in order to be a member of God's family. What is more, Christ has done something on our behalf which we could not do for ourselves. As a result, acceptance with God (justification) comes as a gift through faith in Jesus, apart from the Law.

How could that be? The Jews believed that a broken relationship with God could only be restored through a sacrifice. Paul uses that metaphor when he makes the point here that Christ's death is a sacrifice for sin provided by God in accordance with the Law. This is the divine means of demonstrating God's saving character and opening the door to his family for everyone who believes (vv. 21–26). This powerful image conveys the necessity and cost of Christ's giving of himself on our behalf.

We can summarize the flow of Paul's thought in this way: God's righteousness has now been powerfully revealed not by the Law, but in Christ (v. 21). A restored relationship with God is available to all who trust, for all stand in equal need of that righteousness (vv. 22–23). The gift of justification comes through the redeeming work of Christ, which demonstrates the saving righteousness of God, who had not previously judged sin as it deserved (vv. 24–26). Because it is a gift, and not something that can be accomplished by keeping the Law, justification by faith excludes any possibility of boasting (Paul may be thinking particularly of the Jewish boasts of being a privileged people, vv. 27f.). This does not mean that faith is opposed to the Law. Authentic faith in Christ actually upholds and fulfils the intention of the Law (vv. 29–31), although Paul waits until later in the letter to say how.

6 Abraham's example of faith *Read Romans 4:1–25*

Having stated the bold idea that justification comes through faith in Christ apart from works of the Law, Paul has some explaining to do. He turns to the example of Abraham, the father of the chosen people, to show that he too came to be accepted by God on the basis of grace through faith (v. 2). Conservative Jewish Christians might argue that circumcision, the sign of membership in God's community, was originally given to Abraham, and the custom should be maintained by Gentiles as well as Jews. From what he says later in the letter (and in his epistle to the Galatians), we know that Paul saw the value of circumcision and keeping the Law, but he argues that its purpose was temporary.

The whole chapter consists of an exposition of Genesis 15:6 (see v. 3). Abraham believed God's promise of blessing, and his faith was 'reckoned to him as righteousness'. In other words, he was accepted by God not because he kept certain religious customs, but because he trusted what God said. He took God at his word; when Abraham did so, God considered him to be a righteous man. This means that he was not justified as a debt paid in return for his deeds or observances, but by grace (vv. 4–8). He was not justified by being circumcised (vv. 9–12) or by keeping the Law (which only brings condemnation, vv. 13–15). Instead, as the archetypal person of faith, he was reckoned as righteous by grace (vv. 16–22). This truth confirms that likewise God justifies those who trust in his gracious provision for them in Christ (vv. 23–25).

It is interesting to compare Paul's description of Abraham, the man of faith, with the picture of Abraham we find in Genesis 12–25. For Paul, faith is not an emotion or feeling that comes and goes, sweeping one off into religious fervour. It is a determined reliance upon God that recognizes and gives thanks for his blessings, and looks forward to his provision. Abraham's faith grew through his failures as well as his successes, as he progressively acknowledged God's hand in his life.

GUIDELINES

Sin often begins with an active or passive refusal to honour God. Thanksgiving can be a barometer of spiritual health (1:21): without it, faith atrophies.

> *'Letting us have our own way is not a measure of God's grace, it is the visitation of his wrath. The discipline which does not let us do whatever comes into our heads is not a form of evil, it is the very essence of grace'*

Paul Achtemeier

9–15 SEPTEMBER ROMANS 5:1—8:39

1 Acceptance means hope *Read Romans 5:1–11*

Someone has said that whenever we see a 'therefore' it pays to look closely there to see what it is 'there for'. In this passage Paul begins to talk about the benefits of justification for his readers. The key words are 'through our Lord Jesus Christ'. Instead of being under God's judgment, those who believe have peace with God and hope for the future. There is no longer any boasting in the Law which excludes (2:17, 23; 3:27), but a boasting/rejoicing (vv. 2, 11: the same Greek root is used) because of God's inclusive love revealed through Christ.

The peace that Paul speaks of is not an emotion (although we may rightly feel at peace), but a new relationship with God that does not depend on feelings. Peace (Hebrew: *Shalom*) was a blessing of the covenant (Numbers 6:22–27), and prophets said peace belonged to the age to come (Isaiah 9:6f.; 54:10; Ezekiel 34:25–31). Peace is a reality for Christians now, because we are reconciled to God through Jesus (v. 11).

For Paul, hope means confident expectation rather than wishful thinking. It transforms attitudes so that people can exult (v. 3, again the 'boasting' word) even in afflictions and trials. This confidence is rooted in God's outpoured love, 'like a cloudburst on a parched countryside', known in the gift of his Spirit (vv. 3–5). Justification affects our life today.

Confident hope also has a solid foundation in God's love because he took the initiative while we were still separated from him by sin (vv. 6–8). Paul never ceased to be amazed that God did not wait for people to clean up their lives and become 'deserving' before he acted in Christ to deliver them. On the Damascus road, Paul, like Zacchaeus (Luke 19:1–10), found himself surprised by the grace of God. While he was still a persecutor of the Church, he came to see that Christ had died on his behalf. Justification means forgiveness for our past life.

If Christ's death demonstrates God's love for sinners, his resurrection life assures our future deliverance from any fear of condemnation (vv. 9–10). The future tenses in these verses point to a confidence that physical death is not the end of the story. Because Jesus lives, we shall live. Justification ensures a life to come.

2 A tale of two men *Read Romans 5:12–21*

In this passage Paul points out the results of Christ's death for humanity as a whole. Past, present and future are joined in the two persons of Adam and Christ. Questions about Adam (whose name is the Hebrew word for 'man' in general) and the origin of human sin should not cloud the central truth that Christ has done something all of humanity have failed to do, and by that action God's grace has overcome death. The universal sin and death after Adam has been more than balanced by the fulness of grace and righteousness that has come in Christ.

The passage is particularly difficult because it is written in typical Pauline style—he starts a sentence and gets side-tracked by the size of the issues he raises! He begins a comparison of Christ with Adam in 5:12, digresses in verses 13–14, and emphasizes their contrasting differences in 15–17 before resuming his original comparison in verse 18. We can summarize the main ideas this way: (1) Sin and death have affected all people since Adam's failure (vv. 12–14); (2) By comparison, God's justifying grace has abounded much more through Christ to many (vv. 15–17); (3) Whereas Adam's act of disobedience has led to sin, Christ's obedience has brought righteousness and life (vv. 18–21).

Paul's purpose is to show that the hope in 5:1–11 is a certain one, because just as surely as we share in the reality of sin and death (the consequences of human disobedience), so certainly we will share in the consequences of what Christ has done. By stressing the universality of the effects of Adam's and Christ's actions, the comparison also shows that *all* people—Jews and Gentiles alike—are affected.

Although he asserts a connection, Paul does not explain the link between Adam's sin and ours. Neither does he address why we sin, and many have tried to fill in the gap. He is trying to express that there is a real unity in the human race. We in the West tend to think in terms of individuals; Paul, Judaism and most cultures think in terms of families, groups and corporate identity (so Israel suffered for Achan's sin in Joshua 7). One parent's choices often affect the whole family, for better or for worse. One terrorist can bring a powerful act of destruction to a land that desperately wants peace. This truth has a good side to it: what Christ has done brings a new relationship with God and life to anyone who receives his gift (v. 17).

3 Sin and the Christian *Read Romans 6:1–23*

At the end of his comparison of Christ and Adam, Paul states that although sin increased through the coming of the Law (a claim he will have to explain later in chapter 7), God's grace abounded all the more (5:20). He knows that this is controversial and will provoke questions, so he poses them himself in verses 1 and 15. If it gives grace an opportunity to be seen, why not continue in sin (something Rasputin taught at the time of the Russian revolution)? Paul had raised a similar question in 3:8 but did not answer it; now he does.

We might expect an answer to emphasize the holiness of God, the evil of sin, and the importance of loving others. Certainly Paul believed those things. But here he gives a surprising response. Sin is not an option because, by being baptized into Christ, we have *died* to its hold on us (vv. 1–14). Instead of being enslaved to sin, we who belong to Christ are now *bound* to serve God, inasmuch as we are his and he is our new master (vv. 15–23).

This does not mean that sin is powerless or impossible for the Christian (Paul was quite aware of human nature), but that it is unthinkable. Something decisive has happened to us. Paul is not talking here about the daily dying to sin when we say no to temptation. Jesus himself had spoken of his death as a baptism (Mark 10:38f,; Luke 12:50), and Paul saw in Christian baptism a joining together with Christ in his death. This means that any pre-Christian life that left out God is finished, and we now walk in newness of life, in expectation of one day sharing in Jesus' resurrection.

This leads to the first imperative in the letter to the Romans: we should consider (the same word used of God 'reckoning' Abraham's faith to him as righteousness in 4:3) ourselves dead to sin and alive to God in Christ Jesus (v. 11). In other words, we are to remind ourselves of what is true of us in Christ. This means saying 'no' to sin's reign and yielding ourselves to God (vv. 12–14).

Furthermore, although we are no longer under the Law's jurisdiction, we are not really 'free' to sin. We belong to a new dominion (vv. 15–18). Inevitably people are servants of something (even their own compulsions) or someone. Paul's language here recalls Jesus' teaching that no one can serve two masters (Matthew 6:24) and that whoever sins is its slave (John 8:34–36). Being God's servant reaps a far better return than slavery to sin (vv. 19–23). If the first half of this chapter focuses on *who* we are in Christ, the second emphasizes *whose*. His service is perfect freedom.

4   What about the Law? *Read Romans 7:1–25*

Because he taught that those in Christ are not bound to keep the regulations of the Jewish Law, Paul was often accused by Christian and non-Christian Jews of being an antinomian (i.e. against the Law). In Romans he has already made a number of provocative statements about the Law, and now he tackles the issue directly. His aim here is to show why a Christian is not under the Law. At the same time, he is at pains to emphasize that the Law itself is a good gift from God, but that it is powerless to deliver us.

Using an imperfect analogy of the law of divorce and remarriage in Judaism, Paul explains that the person united with Christ is free from the Law because a death has occurred (vv. 1–6). Because people have been joined to Christ through baptism (see 6:3–4), they too have died to any claim the Law might have on them, and to the condemnation it brings for human failure.

This does not mean that the Law itself is a bad thing. Unlike the early heretic Marcion, Paul does not reject the Old Testament as worthless (see Romans 15:4; 1 Corinthians 10:11). He goes on to argue that the Law is not sin, but that in effect it increases sin, inasmuch as it brings an awareness of what is wrong. As in Romans 6, Paul depicts sin as a powerful force, which exploits the Law as a tool to lead one to death instead of life (vv. 7–13). Experience shows that though good and agreeable to the inner self, the Law cannot free us from sin's power (vv. 14–25).

This is one of the most difficult passages in Romans to interpret. Is Paul speaking autobiographically in verses 7ff.? Many see him echoing the story of Adam in the garden of Eden in verses 7–11. If verses 14–25 are autobiographical, is he referring to his Christian or pre-Christian experience? Both options bristle with difficulties. Clearly Paul is not trying to give a full picture of Christian experience, because he does not bring in the role of the Holy Spirit until chapter 8. It may be that he has in mind the Jewish person without Christ. In any event, he is describing human existence viewed with respect to what the Law can or cannot do. To use a modern analogy, the Law is like a thermometer which can indicate when there is a problem, but unlike a thermostat it can do nothing to change the temperature. Rescue has come in the person of Jesus Christ (v. 25).

F

5 The difference the Spirit makes *Read Romans 8:1–17*

In chapter 8, Paul discusses the nature of the deliverance anticipated in his thanksgiving in 7:25. At the same time, the 'therefore' in 8:1 connects back to 7:6 and the idea of not being under the condemnation of the Law. Viewed in respect to the Law and self, human existence is frustrated by the continuing power of sin. Viewed from another perspective (what God is doing by his Spirit), life is very different. This is the life in which there is freedom (see 2 Corinthians 3:17), the Law is established (Romans 3:31) and its requirement is fulfilled (vv. 4; 13:8–10).

For Paul, the presence of God's Spirit is the *sine qua non* of the Christian. The word Spirit occurs much more often here (twenty-one times) than in any other chapter in the New Testament. This is Paul's most thorough exposition of the work of the Spirit, and the chapter repays careful study. First of all, the Spirit brings freedom for obedience for those who are delivered through Christ's death. A higher 'Law of the Spirit of life' has set us free from any sentence of condemnation, and from bondage brought by sin's use of the Old Testament Law. The sacrificial death of God's Son effected that deliverance, with the aim that Christians now fulfil the Law's original purpose, through the Spirit's power (vv. 1–4).

Secondly, the Spirit enables a new order of existence, in contrast to the old one (vv. 5–11). His presence in our lives means a different agenda (v. 5), and a different result (vv. 6–11). By 'flesh' Paul means human *nature* in its weakness and rebellion against God—he is not implying here that the stuff of which we are made is bad. A flesh-oriented life is hostile to God, powerless and incapable of pleasing him (vv. 7–8). By contrast, because we have the Spirit, we consequently have life now, as well as the prospect of future resurrection (vv. 9–11).

The practical conclusion of God's gift of the Spirit is that we should live by that Spirit, resulting in life (vv. 12–13). The Spirit does more than give life. He leads us (v. 14) and also communicates our new relationship with God, by confirming that we are his children and thus heirs with Christ (vv. 14–17). Paul is careful however to avoid any idea of hollow triumphalism. Being joined to Christ inevitably means suffering with him now, as well as eventually sharing his vindication.

6   Groanings in hope *Read Romans 8:18–39*

After introducing the themes of suffering and glory in 8:17, Paul reflects on the contrast between what is and what will be. His main idea is that in the midst of suffering, our hope for a glorious future can be confident because of (1) the ministry of God's Spirit praying through us; (2) the knowledge that God's ultimate purpose is for good; and (3) the certainty of God's love for us in Christ.

Although we see suffering and decay all around us now, a marvellous future lies ahead not only for God's children, but also for his world. The whole creation that was originally cursed because of Adam's failure (Genesis 3:17–19) will be restored and revitalized along with those in the Last Adam. In the meantime, the creation groans (v. 22) and the Church groans (v. 23) as we long for deliverance and renewal, but the Spirit groans with us as well (v. 26, the same root is used). The Spirit is the first fruits of our hope (v. 23), in the sense that his presence with us is a foretaste and pledge of the fulness of resurrection life. We have not seen what that life shall be like (although we catch glimpses through the love of others), but we wait for it with eagerness. The Spirit enables us to persevere and pray through our difficulties (vv. 26–27). He prays on our behalf in us and through us, which gives us confidence because he knows how to pray—according to the will of God.

Despite the hardships we may experience, that will of God is ultimately for good, and is certainly going to achieve its goal for his people (vv. 28–30). Paul's hope had deep roots in the sovereignty of God. The truth of verse 28 is sometimes impossible for people in the midst of extreme pain to claim, and the verse raises unanswerable questions about evil and the meaning of misery. Nevertheless, it is crucial to remember what Paul had been through when he wrote these words: he was no stranger to suffering (2 Corinthians 11:23–33).

Finally, with a series of rhetorical questions, Paul stirs our hope with words that are often read today at funerals. If God is for us, who will accuse us (vv. 31–33a)? If God says we are righteous, who says we are not (vv. 33b–34a)? If Christ loves us, what can separate us from that love (vv. 34b–37)? This passage forms the climax of the larger section, chapters 6–8.

GUIDELINES

Some thoughts arising out of this week's readings:

- *Paul considered himself to be a dead man when it came to sin. This did not mean that he saw himself as perfect; no doubt he confessed his failings as we all do. But instead of being preoccupied with his sin and expecting to fail, he set his sights on Another and on his calling to serve. For him, sin was unthinkable. James taught that we cave in to sin when we allow it to be an option by entertaining the possibility (James 1:14f.). We are what we think, and what we set our minds on shapes what we become (Philippians 4:8f.).*

- *Some people on a beach one summer laughed in ridicule when they saw a young man wearing a T-shirt saying 'I'm a fool for Christ'—until, that is, they read on the back of his shirt, 'Whose fool are you?'*

- *How do we know that the Holy Spirit is at work in us? We may not have the spectacular experiences of some, but whenever we cry out to God as our Father, we can know that it is that very Spirit prompting us (8:15f.). When we are at a complete loss for words to express the perplexity, pain or desire of our hearts in prayer, the Spirit is at work interceding for us (8:26f.).*

16–22 SEPTEMBER   ROMANS 9:1—12:21

1   God's freedom to choose *Read Romans 9:1–29*

Some have thought that Romans 9–11 form a parenthesis which could be skipped without affecting the letter's power. Nothing could be further from the truth. The ideas of God's purpose (8:28) and his love (8:39) inseparably link this section with what precedes. In three chapters Paul wrestles with his biggest theological problem—God's faithfulness to his beloved people, the Jews.

Paul has asserted that God is impartial: with regard to salvation there is no difference between Jew and Gentile since both are justified by grace through faith in Christ. By removing circumcision and the Law as requirements for salvation, Paul has stripped the Jewish people of their prime distinctives. And by insisting on salvation through Jesus, he has apparently excluded the majority of Jews from the kingdom of God. How can this be reconciled with God's calling of and promises to Israel? Where is the justice and covenant faithfulness of God? Paul must deal with the issue at length, not only for his Jewish readers, but also for the Gentile Christians, who evidently were susceptible to anti-Semitic sentiments prevalent in Rome. Ultimately Paul will respond that Israel's rejection of God's righteousness in Christ, though deliberate, is according to God's merciful plan and only temporary.

He begins by affirming how tragic Israel's rejection of Christ is (vv. 1–5). Paul deeply grieved for his people (vv. 1–3), and the Jews have so many blessings from God (vv. 4–5). But Paul stresses that God's word to them has not failed, because being a member of his people is not a matter of physical lineage but of gracious divine choice (vv. 6–13). With a promise God *chose* Isaac and his offspring to be his children (vv. 6–9), and he went on to *choose* Jacob apart from anything Jacob had done (vv. 10–13). He is free to have mercy on whomever he chooses, apart from human choice or action, and he can even harden whomever he wants to in order to accomplish his good will (vv. 14–18). This raises the question of human responsibility, but Paul stubbornly refuses to surrender God's sovereignty on the altar of human freedom: creatures cannot dictate to their Creator. God does not have to answer to us (vv. 19–21)!

At this point the modern reader may be tempted to reject Paul's seemingly capricious God. But so far, we have only heard part of the overall argument. Paul stresses divine freedom here in order to help his conservative Jewish readers to see that God is free to *broaden* and *extend* his kindness to Gentiles. Paul finds in Hosea a prophecy that God will include Gentiles in his mercy, whereas Isaiah had warned that only a remnant will be saved—the present situation has been prophesied (vv. 23–29).

2 Responsible to trust *Read Romans 9:30—10:21*

Although he has stressed divine election in 9:1–29, Paul has no intention of denying human responsibility. He affirms these two apparently contradictory truths without compromising God's sovereignty or human dignity. According to today's reading, Israel is fully responsible for its rejection of God's righteousness in Christ.

It is important to understand here that Paul is not condemning Judaism *per se*, but grieving over the Jews' conscious rejection of the good news that Jesus is the Messiah. When he states that Gentiles have received God's righteousness but Jews have mistakenly pursued their own righteousness through works of the Law, Paul is not characterizing historic Judaism as a religion in which one earns salvation (a common and seriously mistaken caricature). Old Testament faith was based on the grace of God just as much as New Testament belief: we have seen that Abraham was Paul's prime example (ch. 4). When Paul speaks of 'faith' now, however, he specifically means 'trust in Christ'.

Paul is describing what the Jews' insistence on keeping the Law *instead of trusting in Christ* amounted to. When they rejected Jesus, their pursuit of a right relationship with God through his Law became a detour from the 'obedience of faith' (1:5). Instead of leading them to its goal (Christ), the Law became an end in itself (v. 4). Paul is not talking here about individual Jews who have never heard of Jesus, but about the people as a whole to whom he had preached so often without success.

The Old Testament testifies to the righteousness of faith, and the gospel that brings this right relationship with God is just as accessible as the Law (vv. 5–13). It must be heard to be believed (vv. 14–15). Many Jewish people heard but did not respond to the preaching of the gospel (vv. 16–18). Even Gentiles understood and trusted, but Israel stubbornly resisted (vv. 19–21), as they had before in scripture. Still, this is not the end of the story...

3 A purpose in jealousy *Read Romans 11:1–36*

After painting a bleak picture for Israel in chapters 9–10, Paul sketches a scene of hope. Their widespread lack of trust in Jesus will not thwart the divine plan to bless them and all peoples. A remnant remains even now (those Jews who claim Jesus as the Christ), chosen by grace (vv. 1–7a). The rest of Israel has stumbled in unbelief by not accepting the Messiah (vv. 7b–10), but with the failure of the Jewish mission the door is open for the reconciliation of the world through the Gentile mission (compare Acts 13:46f.).

God is not finished with Israel (vv. 11–16). Paul looks for a day when divine inclusion of the Gentiles will make Jewish people jealous of God's mercy and bring them back to Jesus. Paul hints here at something expressed again in verses 25–26. But before that, his concern for the attitude of his non-Jewish readers bursts through in verses 17–24. Using the metaphor of an olive tree Paul warns the Gentile Christians in Rome, who are now members of the people of God (wild branches grafted into the tree). They are not to boast or consider themselves superior to the Jews, who as natural branches were 'broken off' for their unbelief. The proper attitude of the Gentiles is not pride or arrogance, but the fear of God (v. 20), remembering the importance of the obedience that proceeds from faith. If Gentiles could be grafted into a tree to which they did not naturally belong, the 'natural' branches could even more easily be expected to be grafted in again.

Such is Paul's hope, expressed in verses 25–27, that at the return of the Messiah all Israel (probably a reference to Jews alive at the time) will repent and claim Christ as their own, so that God's mercy would be seen to extend to all peoples, Jews and Gentiles alike. Paul can only respond to this vision of world reconciliation by marvelling at the wonder of God's wisdom and plan, concluding with a doxology of praise in verse 36.

Unfortunately, Paul's vision remains unrealized, and his warning unheeded. Instead of prompting Jewish people to a constructive 'jealousy' through the mercy of God reflected in their lives, Gentile followers of Jesus have often assumed that they have permanently replaced the Jews as God's family. We have a legacy of anti-Semitic attitudes and persecution to overcome. This does not mean blanket approval of everything the current nation of Israel does. Neither does it mean that the Jews should be denied a hearing of the good news of Jesus. Compassion and appreciation for our shared heritage are in order.

4 The great reversal *Read Romans 12:1–2*

We come at last to the major hinge or turning point in Romans. The 'therefore' in verse 1 looks back over the vista of God's mercies in Christ described in the preceding eleven chapters. Now Paul will describe the behaviour of both Jew and Greek as the one people of God in Christ. Before he outlines right conduct he summarizes the new perspective for a Christian's attitude toward life. These two important verses serve as a heading for the next two chapters.

The *motivation* for our life is thankfulness in response to the mercy we have experienced through Jesus. This gives us a new *perspective*, as we see all of our life as worship (self-offering) in Christ. The *means* by which this is to be accomplished is through an ongoing process of transformation, as our way of thinking (which controls our acting) is renewed by God's Spirit. The *goal* of our life now is faithful obedience to God's perfect will.

Paul's language recalls themes we met earlier in the letter, and particularly the notion of presenting ourselves to God (6:12f., 16, 19). Many also see here a contrast between the living sacrifice offered in Christian worship and the Old Testament practice of animal sacrifice. What they often miss is that Paul is calling us to participate in a great reversal of the downward spiral he described in 1:18–32:

wrath of God (1:18)	*mercies of God*
refusal to honour or thank God (1:21)	*(thankful) pleasing sacrifice*
dishonouring the body (1:26–28)	*offering the body in obedience*
foolish, idolatrous worship (1:21f., 25)	*spiritual worship*
debased mind (1:28)	*renewed mind*
disobeying the decree of God (1:32)	*approving the will of God*

The worship which people failed to offer by refusing to honour God or give thanks (1:21) is now restored through Christ. Paul wants those who have died with Jesus through baptism to join him in offering themselves completely—in effect, after Christ's example. The giving up of Jesus' body as a sacrifice for the sake of others (1 Corinthians 11:24) enables this reversal and provides the pattern for Christian self-offering here. Paul defines worship here not as something that happens only on a Sunday, but as a whole way of life.

5 Responsibility in the body *Read Romans 12:3–8*

Paul now begins to outline some characteristics of the transformed life. From right thinking about one's relationship to God (12:1–2), he turns to right thinking about oneself in verses 3–8. We have already seen that Paul was concerned about Gentile Christians' pride and arrogance towards the Jews (11:17–22), and in chapters 14–15 Paul will address a particular problem dividing Jewish and Gentile Christian groups in Rome. Here he wants the Roman believers to view themselves as interdependent parts of a whole, the body of Christ (vv. 4–5; see also 1 Corinthians 12).

All are important, and have a part to play. Members should measure themselves according to their own faithfulness in fulfilling their God-given role by using their gift(s) as they were intended (vv. 6–8). In other words, a Christian's sense of achievement is not based on how attractive, brilliant, spiritual, wealthy or gifted he or she is, but on a different standard. The important question is, 'How am I *using* my "measure of faith" (v. 3, probably a reference to one's spiritual gifts) for the building up of God's people?'

Paul states the sort of gifts he has in mind in verses 6–8, but as in 1 Corinthians 12:8–10, 28–30 and Ephesians 4:11f. there is no attempt to be comprehensive. Translating the Greek text behind these verses is difficult because the main verb is missing. The New Revised Standard Version turns verse 6 into a statement followed by a list ('We have gifts that differ according to the grace given to us:....'), but the New International Version and the Authorized Version are probably more accurate in preserving the implied imperative that each gift is to be *used* in the way expressed.

The gift of prophecy (more a forth-telling or a sharing of God's perspective than a foretelling) should be exercised in proportion to one's faith. A gift of 'ministry' (literally, 'service'; the root of our

English word 'deacon') should be exercised in actual service, and so on. The mention of the gifts of giving and of compassion ('showing mercy') do not often receive much attention in modern discussions of the gifts of the Spirit, but they are just as vital to the life of God's people as any other.

6 Love in action *Read Romans 12:9–21*

When Paul finishes his words about spiritual gifts and how they are to be used, he turns to the question of Christian behaviour, in general. In our English Bibles, verses 9–21 read like a string of rapid-fire commands ('Do this, don't do that'), and Paul seems quite bossy! But in the Greek text most of the phrases are not so much direct imperatives that *prescribe* behaviour but participles that *describe* it. For instance, verse 12 literally says, 'rejoicing in hope, persevering in affliction, devoting yourselves to prayer' and so forth. Instead of piling up a load of orders to do this or that, Paul is quickly sketching out the rough outlines of a picture of Christian attitudes and conduct. Some of the things he says come from the Old Testament and perhaps a few expressions came from his training as a Pharisee, but his picture of the transformed life looks very much like Jesus.

In verses 9–13 Paul talks about our relations towards fellow Christians; in verses 14–21 he deals primarily with how we are to act towards those outside the faith. His language has many parallels elsewhere, and may have been part of an early Christian catechetical code (training for those newly baptized). The theme holding both sections together is genuine (literally, 'unhypocritical') love (v. 9a).

Distinctively, Christian living is known by the quality of its love. It is a discerning love that is not blind or sentimental, but knows how to distinguish between good and evil. A family kind of love, it includes all in the community of faith (v. 10). Paul describes a zealous, diligent love that burns with the power of the Spirit and whose aim is service (v. 11). Despite setbacks, a life characterized by God's love rejoices in confident hope and perseveres in suffering with prayer (v. 12). Christians are givers (after the image of our Creator), and although hospitality was especially important in Paul's day (v. 13; see the Guidelines section), it remains a powerful and essential mark of love today.

Echoing the words of Jesus, Paul's call to bless and not to curse those who persecute requires real transformation. Genuine love requires more than self-restraint and kindness through clenched teeth. It means not only weeping with the misfortunes of those who weep, but also rejoicing with others when envy might normally be our response. Superior attitudes are replaced by seeking peace, which is possible on our part if we choose not to avenge ourselves and leave room for God. An old Egyptian ritual in which a penitent carried coals in a container on his head as a sign of remorse helps explain verse 20. Surprising kindness when retaliation is expected can melt a heart.

GUIDELINES

The idea of God's choice is a theme that runs through virtually every book of the Bible. This 'scandal of particularity' often leads modern readers to ask, 'What about those not chosen?', as though fallen humanity has a claim on God. By contrast, the original readers would have marvelled at the idea that God chose *anyone* who had rejected him (5:7–8). The early Church found great comfort in the notion that God (as well as humans) had plans, and the doctrine of election was intended to promote humility, confidence and thankfulness, rather than any sense of superiority.

Hospitality was crucial in the first century when there were no church buildings and Christians met in each others' homes. Christian travellers were not keen to spend the night in an inn which was often a brothel. The text of 12:13 literally says 'pursue' hospitality; that meant not simply being willing to put up with the inconvenience of accommodating others, but actually seeking out those who need a place to stay. Our faith calls us to have an open hand, an open heart and an open door.

1   Rendering what is due *Read Romans 13:1–7*

Seeking peace and not revenge with all people has implications for
how we relate to ruling powers. Recognizing that civil authority is
established by God, Christians should live in submission to the
governing authorities. These verses have often been misused
through the centuries, however, to justify unjust government and
to suppress dissent. Several points are important to remember.

First, the belief that all authority and power is ultimately
derived from God was a basic teaching of Judaism (Jeremiah 27:5;
Daniel 4:17; 2 Samuel 12:8; Proverbs 8:15–16, etc.) which Paul
inherited. The first-century Jewish historian Josephus wrote, 'No
ruler attains his office save by the will of God' (*Wars* 2.140). What
an individual ruler or magistrate *does* with that authority is his or
her own responsibility, for which they must one day give an
account to God. Paul is not saying that anything a ruler does is
right. God's gifts are often abused.

Secondly, Paul was a Roman citizen and had seen civil
government come to his aid more than once by the time he wrote
this. Although Jewish Christians (including Priscilla and Aquila)
had been expelled from Rome in AD49, the Roman authorities had
not persecuted Christians widely yet. Paul was writing to a
particular situation in time, and not intending to write a complete
treatise to survey every possible eventuality throughout history.
Roman historians tell us that there was general unrest there during
the 50s over unfair practices of tax collectors. This may provide
the main reason for Paul's words here (vv.6f.): he did not want
Christians to gain the reputation of being lawbreakers, thereby
undermining their testimony to Christ.

Thirdly, in Paul's day Christians were a tiny, powerless minority
who had no political chance of changing the ruling structures.
There was no possibility (or even the idea) of democracy at the
time. Given our opportunities to make a difference today, Paul
would certainly applaud Christian involvement in the political
process to help effect justice and peace.

Finally, from the earliest days, Christians were prepared to disobey orders from authorities if those orders meant disobeying God's command to share the good news of Jesus (Acts 4:19–20). Paul is describing government as it ought to function, in its capacity to correct evil and to reward what is good. When it goes astray, an appropriate non-violent response is in order.

2 Love and expectation *Read Romans 13:8–14*

Paul now begins to summarize his general words about Christian behaviour. He comes back to the theme of love (vv. 8–10), and reminds us that the expectation of Christ's return gives urgency to Christian living (vv. 11–14).

Addressing Christians divided by scruples (see 14:1ff.), Paul insists that love is a lasting debt to others that can never be fully repaid. The unstated reason for this is God's forgiving love towards us (see Ephesians 5:2; Matthew 18:23–35; Luke 7:36–50). His teaching that love for the neighbour fulfils the Law reveals Paul's concern not to reject absolutely his Jewish heritage. It also shows us again how similar his message is to that of Jesus (Mark 12:28–34; Matthew 22:34–40; 5:17). Both find in Leviticus 19:18 the essence of our responsibility towards others.

Although Paul eventually came to accept that he might die before the return of Jesus, he continued to long for and look forward to the second coming. No one knows when it will arrive, but each day brings that day nearer, making the present a time to be alert (vv. 11–12a). Readiness does not mean scanning the sky, but a refusal to slumber by being conformed to this world (12:2), succumbing to the anaesthetizing delusions of this age (see 1 Thessalonians 5:5–8). Instead, Christians are called to put away the old way of life that leaves God out, and to live honourably as those who reflect Christ's character (vv. 12b–14).

What we wear says something to the world about who we are. To 'put on the Lord Jesus Christ' (v. 14) is to clothe ourselves with him, to don his characteristics. Elsewhere Paul says that Christians have already put on the 'new self' (Colossians 3:10), which is being renewed after the image of Christ (2 Corinthians 3:18; 4:4). When Paul speaks of clothing ourselves with compassion, kindness, humility, meekness and so on in Colossians 3:12ff., these characteristics come from a stock of descriptions applied to Jesus.

3 A problem: the weak and the strong *Read Romans 14:1–23*

Apparently, Jewish Christians and Gentile Christians in Rome were divided. They differed over whether one should abstain from eating meat that was ceremonially unclean according to Jewish Law (v. 2), observe Jewish religious days (v. 5), and (probably) abstain from wine (some of which may have been poured out in honour of the gods, v. 21). This was fundamentally a religious difference, based on what Christians believed was right before God.

The weak (mostly Jewish believers) were in the minority. When they returned to Rome after being expelled by Claudius in AD49, they faced a difficult situation. They could not go back to worshipping in synagogues without being forced to renounce Christ: it was arguments in the synagogues over Jesus that had caused them to be expelled from Rome in the first place. Neither could they easily join in worship with the 'strong' Gentile Christians whose religious liberty threatened their traditions. If they worshipped with the strong, the weak would be tempted to compromise their convictions because of the arguments and confidence of the strong, some of whom despised their 'narrow' customs. The weak were also tempted to respond by 'passing judgment on' (i.e. condemning) the strong as pleasing only themselves and not being obedient to God.

In 14:1—15:13 Paul seeks to help a liberal majority (the strong) and a conservative minority (the weak) to live together in peace. He urges the strong to welcome the weak, but not in order to argue with them. He reminds the weak that God has accepted their more liberal fellow Christians, and that the weak are not their masters (6:3f.). Although we know that Paul himself agrees with the convictions of the strong (15:1), he does not try to persuade the weak that their customs are mistaken. Instead, he urges all to be fully convinced in their own minds (so that they will act from faith, instead of fear). He reminds them that both groups are seeking to honour one Lord in their convictions, and neither has a monopoly on piety (vv. 6–8). Jesus' death and resurrection mean that both groups belong to him, and both will give an answer on judgment day, not to each other, but to God (vv. 9–12). Both should give up attitudes that reflect superiority in passing judgment on the other (v. 13a).

From verse 13b Paul concentrates on the strong. He urges them to refrain from exercising their liberty to eat meat in the presence of the weak if it leads those more conservative Christians to spiritual ruin (by tempting them to compromise their faith). The welfare of the weak should be more important than the appetites of the strong. Responsibilities take priority over rights.

4 A strategy and vision for unity *Read Romans 15:1–13*

Paul's strategy for unity for the Roman Christians is similar to that in Philippians 2:1–11. He calls them back to the supreme example of the one who came to unite them. In particular, Paul points them to Jesus' humility and love, seen in three specific respects.

First, the strong should bear the weaknesses (the NRSV's 'put up with the failings' is not as positive as the Greek text) of the weak, and not please themselves by flaunting their religious liberty. If the strong were to refrain from eating meat when they shared meals with the weak, this could lead to ridicule from their fellow Gentiles. That would not be easy to endure. But Christ did not please himself; he bore reproach from others in obedience to God, just as the psalmist had done (Psalm 69:7–9). Paul prays that God who is the source of the kind of endurance and encouragement prompted in scripture will grant them unity (v. 5).

Secondly, Jesus' free acceptance of sinners, his welcoming of others to himself, provides the pattern for the strong's reception of the weak and vice versa (v. 7). The verb Paul uses here is identical to that in 14:1. Paul probably has in mind not only the weak and the strong but also their reception of Phoebe, who will be bringing the letter (16:1–2).

Thirdly, Christ became a servant of the Jews (the circumcised, v. 8) in order to fulfil two ends: (1) to confirm the promises made by the (Jewish) patriarchs; and, (2) so that the Gentiles should glorify God for his mercy (see 11:30). If Jesus was a servant to the Jews, how can the 'strong' refrain from doing the same for their 'weak' brethren? And if he became a servant so that ultimately Gentiles might be included in God's family, how can the 'weak' complain about their eating habits?

In verses 9b–12 Paul supports his claim in 12:9a by showing from scripture that the vision of Jew and Gentile joining together in praise to God should be no surprise. Now he summarizes the concern of his letter and of his ministry to the Gentiles. With its themes of hope, joy, peace, faith and the power of the Spirit, this section gathers together his desire for his readers in a prayer, providing a fitting climax.

F

5 Reasons for writing and final plans *Read Romans 15:14–33*

Having finished the gist of his message to the Romans, Paul now steps back and reflects on why he has written and what he hopes to do. Diplomatically, he praises his readers' understanding and explains his own boldness of speech because of his responsibility to serve the Gentiles (vv. 14–16). He must be careful not to be presumptuous in his strong words to people he has never visited before.

Paul has not come to Rome before, because until now his work has meant preaching in a wide arc between Jerusalem and Illyricum (modern Serbia, Croatia, Albania). His language sounds grandiose, as though he himself has evangelized the entire area (v. 23). From the evidence of Acts and the letters, Paul apparently saw his primary task as establishing churches in urban centres and setting his converts loose to preach to outlying regions. The expectation that Christ might return soon impelled him to travel widely.

We do not know for certain whether Paul's plans to preach in Spain (v. 24) were fulfilled. Ancient traditions say that he did go there, but if Acts is accurate Paul must have been released from his imprisonment in Rome and executed after a second imprisonment there. Paul's main purpose in writing Romans clearly appears in verses 14f., 28f. (see the Introduction above).

Paul's trip to Jerusalem with relief money collected from Christians in Macedonia and Greece indicates his desire to meet practical needs and to demonstrate the solidarity of Gentile and Jewish followers of Jesus (vv. 25–27). Nevertheless, his arrival in the place where Jesus was crucified will be fraught with danger, leading Paul to ask for the prayers of the Romans (vv. 30–32). Just as he once persecuted Christians, he will risk death at the hands of fellow Jews. We can hear his anxiety about his reception by the conservative Jewish Christians there when he asks for prayer that his ministry to Jerusalem 'may be acceptable to the saints' (v. 31). His concern was well founded. As Acts records, Paul was taken into custody there and was kept in captivity at Caesarea before being sent as a prisoner to Rome.

6 Final greetings and goodbye *Read Romans 16:1–27*

Chapter 16 is missing from some ancient manuscripts of Romans. Luther felt that Paul would not have ended such a magnificent epistle with a list of names! The manuscript evidence, however, overwhelmingly supports its inclusion, and the shorter versions of Romans probably arose from a desire to increase its appeal to a wider audience.

The list offers us an important clue to Paul's success as an apostle. He was not an ideologue; he valued people, cultivated friendships and praised his co-workers. Here we meet Phoebe, a 'deacon' (probably referring to a specific responsibility, see Philippians 1:1) from the community at Cenchreae, a seaport near Corinth. She was a person of some wealth (12:2), and carried Paul's letter to the Romans.

Prisc(ill)a and Aquila also receive fulsome praise from Paul, and we know them from Acts 18:2, 18, 26; 1 Corinthians 16:19; and 2 Timothy 4:19. They too were fairly wealthy, and had worked with Paul in Corinth and Ephesus. Prisc(ill)a appears first in most of the references to the couple, causing many commentators to suspect that she was the dominant partner.

Three more individuals mentioned here are particularly interesting. Junia in verse 7 is almost certainly a reference to a woman, and she is called 'prominent among the apostles' and 'in Christ' before Paul came to faith. She and her husband Andronicus have Greek names but were Jews ('my relatives'), and may well have been among Peter's audience at Pentecost: Luke tells us that people from Rome were in the crowd (Acts 2:10). Although his name was fairly common, Rufus (v. 13) could have been the son of Simon of Cyrene, who carried Jesus' cross. Mark's Gospel, written probably in Rome, records that Simon was 'the father of Alexander and Rufus' (Mark 15:21). Finally, verse 22 reminds us that Paul did not write the letter to the Romans— Tertius did. It was Paul's practice to dictate to a secretary.

Paul's list in chapter 16 mentions twenty-nine people, twenty-seven of them by name. It is striking that fully a third of these persons were women. Clearly the common view that Paul devalued women and their ministry needs to be revised!

GUIDELINES

Although the issues dividing conservative and more liberal Christians today are different from those separating the weak and strong believers in Rome, Paul's strategy for unity is just as relevant for us. We share a common Lord and will all give account to him one day. We would do well to recognize that, on our better days, all Christians seek to be faithful to the light we have from God, and to give each other the benefit of the doubt.

Caricaturing those who differ, and provoking them by emphasizing those practices and beliefs which divide us, is not the way forward. We all can do with the reminder that the kingdom of God is righteousness, peace and joy in the Holy Spirit (14:17). But even more importantly, we find our unity only in the person of Jesus Christ, whose Lordship unites us. When we adopt his example of self-denying service, it becomes impossible to act superior, to pass judgment or to ridicule the views of others.

Further reading

John Stott, *The Message of Romans*, Inter-Varsity Press, 1994

Michael B. Thompson, *Clothed with Christ: The Example and Teaching of Jesus in Romans 12:1—15:13*, JSNT, Sheffield Academic Press, 1991 (from which some of the material in these notes has been adapted, with permission)

John Ziesler, *Paul's Letter to the Romans*, SCM Press, 1989

Ecclesiastes

As one enters the City Museum and Art Gallery in Birmingham one comes to an extremely large painting—*February Fill Dyke*, 1881, by B.W. Leader. Sombre colours, clouds, bare trees, sodden fields, muddy ways around the cottages—all could give, at first, a dismal impression. But then one notes the gleams of light in the sky and on the patches of water, and one feels how the wet of February is the necessary precursor to the joy of spring. Sombre and subdued though it is, the picture has its own beauty, and one may come to love it deeply.

The painting sets us on the way to appreciate Ecclesiastes. Here is a little book, hovering between poetry and prose, written in Hebrew in about the third century BC, which declares again and again that all is *hebel*—vanity, futility, emptiness, and passing as a puff of air. And yet we are drawn to read these grave thoughts as generations have done before, and like them we may yet find here beauty, wisdom and peace.

The unknown writer has given his words dramatic form, like a play for one actor. Onto his stage he brings the ancient king Solomon, legendary for wisdom and wealth. He has him reflect on what he has found, on great endeavours that have proved empty, and on humble ways that have surprised with joy.

The greatest biblical scholar of the early Church, Origen, greatly valued Ecclesiastes as an aid to union with God. The three books ascribed to Solomon, he thought, corresponded to the three stages of the soul's journey: Proverbs gave the moral basis, teaching the renunciation of evil ways; Ecclesiastes revealed the insubstantial nature of worldly life, preparing the soul for true and lasting value; the Song of Songs finally brought the soul into loving union with the Lord.

We too, as we read Ecclesiastes, will be gaining a preparation, travelling through quiet reflections and reassessments towards the only place of true and lasting value, our home with God.

No particular version is referred to here, but it should be noted that our English translations occasionally differ widely due to difficulties in the original.

1   The lost meaning *Read Ecclesiastes 1*

The sayings are presented as from 'Kohelet, son of David, king in Jerusalem'. The figure of Solomon is somewhat veiled by this name or title '(the) Kohelet', for which the Greek translators put 'Ecclesiastes' ('member of the assembly') and English Bibles usually have 'the Preacher' or 'the Teacher'. It may be an old title for the kind of 'convenor' (and so president and speaker) of the national assembly for worship. Or it may describe the sage-king as the supreme 'collector', who assembled a vast array of wise proverbs. In either case, here is one familiar with the best of wisdom.

And this is the character who now declares, with the utmost emphasis, that he has found all human toil and trouble to be for nothing. It is all utter *hebel*, he says, and will say again often. The word means 'vapour', 'breath', 'puff of air', and then what is quickly passing, without substance or enduring value. Our English Bibles have 'vanity', 'futility', 'emptiness', '(what is) meaningless'. The haunting refrain of *hebel* throughout the book signals the bafflement of human understanding. Considering what humankind achieves with all its busy efforts and ambitions, this wisest and most experienced of minds concludes that it is all in vain, evanescent, for nothing.

But our sage sings a beautiful lament over this sorry condition. In the mighty course of nature's elements he finds images of comings and goings, of outings and returnings that lead nowhere. The sun ever rises and sets, the wind moves round and back, the waters too pass round and round. So man sees and hears, never finding satisfaction, never finally achieving, never reaching the 'new' territory where the striving would be fulfilled. The hoped-for 'new' is only the old, disguised, and we are back on the treadmill of pointless effort.

How like our own age, when 'Solomon' reflects that he amassed knowledge and surpassed in understanding all that went before— and yet at the end it was all like 'chasing the wind' (or better, 'herding the wind')—much effort all in vain. Heavy and exhausting the labour of study, and distressing its conclusions! The more knowledge, the more pain.

Not the whole story, we may object. But let us abide for a while in this valley of sad realism, where the noise of the world's business becomes a hollow echo, and then silence.

2   Experiment in living *Read Ecclesiastes 2*

The philosopher-king tells us how he experimented with the options for living. As a young man might, he first tried the way of merry-making; pleasure and fun beckoned to him. Soon he felt he needed to go further, and drank much wine in a calculated effort to find the elusive satisfaction.

He attained the age when the heart is set on property. He had various residences built, and on the sunny hillsides he made terraced vineyards. He devised enclosed gardens and parks, skilfully made with reservoirs and channels to nurture every kind of fruit tree. For all this property he acquired a great array of male and female servants. His herds of cattle and flocks of sheep and goats were more numerous than those of preceding kings. He amassed royal treasures of gold, silver and precious stones. In his palaces skilled singers, male and female, sang to the plucked strings. (The end of v. 8 has been thought to refer to concubines or kinds of instruments, but the Hebrew is obscure.) And with all this solid evidence of royal greatness there continued his fame as supreme philosopher and life-manager, the one who understood the way to achievement.

Yet when he took stock of it all, it seemed to him nothing but *hebel*, a pointless herding of the wind, vain endeavour that yielded no lasting profit. Then he generalized from his experience. Anyone seeking to do great works after Solomon could scarcely surpass him. There was no solution along that path. He could grant the general opinion that wisdom was better than folly, as light surpassed the darkness. But where was the difference in the end? Death and forgetting came to fools and wise men alike. ('You find two skulls on an ancient ruin,' a Babylonian author had said a thousand years earlier, 'and can you say which was the wise man, which the fool?') All the threads of the wise king's thoughts led to a sorrowful conclusion. For all the toil of life's day and all the anxieties of the night, there was in the end nothing to show.

Yet despite the wave of pessimism that has swept over our speaker, some positive gleams appear again (vv. 24–26): where God is mentioned, how can all value be denied to life? From his hand something good will be received. In simple living—eating and drinking, working and laughing—God gives wisdom and joy. The vanishing of great riches will be a sorrow to the one who wrongly set his heart on them (v. 25 should probably end: 'apart from *him*, a reading generally adopted in our English Bibles).

3 The shifts of experience *Read Ecclesiastes 3*

To know the right thing to do or the right thing to speak in a particular time was considered a mark of great wisdom. But our speaker's theme here is different. It concerns the contrasting kinds of experience which fall to us by God's appointment. We must expect to have allotted to us, he says, times of sorrow and times of joy. When we accept this and consider it deeply, we shall see more steadily and soberly into the human condition. (It is not clear if v. 5a refers to something specific.)

After the poem on the contrasting experiences allotted to us, verse 9 seems to begin again the lamenting of the human situation. But there are some remarkable sayings in the following verses. God 'has made everything beautiful in its time', just right for its moment. And 'he has put the *olam*, in their heart, yet not that man should be able to discover the work God has done from beginning to end.' This *olam* 'eternity/world', seems to denote a great span of memory and hope, an instinct for the remote past and future, which yet falls short of comprehending the whole range of God's work. Wonderful as is the gift of imaginative intelligence, it must be matched by the humility to know its limitations before God. There will be something good for the realistically humble life (v. 12), which finds happiness where it is given and always looks to do good. Eating and drinking represent simple, basic things in life, along with vigorous work. There is happiness in finding in these the gifts of God.

In reverence for God (vv. 14–15) there is an immense depth of peace. The flux of time, the shocks of catastrophes—all become still in the contemplation of the eternal perfection in him and in all his works. It is a perfection which comprehends the tragedies of this world. In those very things that seem awry ('driven away/persecuted'), he is at work, seeking and saving.

This wonderful insight is that of one who looks realistically at the world (vv. 16–22). He sees that people responsible for justice are themselves corrupt. On man and beasts the hand of death falls alike, the coldness and decay are the same. This much is seen, and who can distinguish the destination of their spirits? The modest portion of earthly life, the simple fare and labour, that is where happiness can be found. And that is where, against all the odds, the knowledge of God's perfection can possess us and bring peace.

4 Competition versus cooperation *Read Ecclesiastes 4*

The sage now looks more closely at society and notes especially examples of wrong. Oh, the tears of the mistreated! And none to defend and restore them from the power of their oppressors! He has seen so much of this cruelty that he must exclaim that it is better to be dead, better still never to have been born.

We hear more reflections on toil. On the one hand, work—and clever work too—is often done only to outdo a neighbour. On the other hand, the fool who is idle wastes his life. It is better to work without greed or envy: 'better a handful with peace of mind, than two fists full with toil that is herding the wind.'

Some are so greedy for riches that they toil away although they have no family to provide for. Two at least can work for each other and help each other in time of trouble. Cooperation is good, 'and a threefold cord is not quickly broken'.

Only too familiar in our day is the instance of the folly in society given in verses 13–16. An old ruler no longer listens to advice. A young man rises against him, and emerges from imprisonment and poverty to be triumphant. All go wild for the new ruler; optimism is unbounded. But when his turn comes to be succeeded, his failures too are apparent, and wretched is the memory of his rule.

(In most of our Bibles chapter 4 ends with verse 16, while in a few it includes the next verse. There will thus be a difference also in the verse numbers of chapter 5.)

5   Quiet in the dwelling of God *Read Ecclesiastes 5*

'Keep your foot'—go carefully, realizing what you are about—
'when you go to the house of God.' You are going to 'hear'—in
obedience; not to offer some contribution which conceals the fact
that you are following your own devices. 'God is in heaven...':
realize that God is God, awesome, infinite, while you are a
creature among creatures, so 'let your words be few'. 'A dream
comes with a multitude of business': when you are hasty and over-
active, you easily becomes unrealistic, carried away with your self-
important ideas. Be thoughtful in what you promise God, so that
you can sincerely try to fulfil your promise and not have to make
excuses (to God, or to the 'messenger', the temple official). Let
plans and words be stilled before the mighty God.

While king and people should fairly share the yield of the land
(vv. 8–9), much injustice occurs through the tiers of management,
the layers of bureaucracy, where each is sucking out advantage for
himself (vv. 7–8). The love of money is never sated. Much wealth
increases dependents and anxieties, and over-indulgence ruins
health and sleep. And how quickly wealth can vanish through
misfortune or misjudgment!

So our sage returns to his counsel that we should be satisfied
with the fundamental and simple things God gives us, glad of our
food and drink and work as we receive our portion from the hands
of God. If the portion is wealth, all the more reason to be aware of
the giver and not put our trust in the things themselves. We are to
live in the present moment, not fret at the passing away of our
time, finding God's answer to our needs in the happiness of our
heart.

6   Plenty but no satisfaction *Read Ecclesiastes 6*

The sage laments the cases where all seems set for enjoyment, but
somehow the chance slips away. He thinks first of someone to
whom God has given wealth and honour. When God does not
decree that he should continue in this prosperity, it all passes into
the hands of a stranger. It is a bitter disappointment, a severe
suffering.

Some praise the value of having a large family and a long life.

But if there is calamity at the end, bringing a wretched old age and not even a proper burial, it would have been better to have died at the outset and never seen the sun. When it comes to remaining alive, the wise man cannot be sure of having any advantage over the foolish or the destitute (v. 8). You may as well be satisfied with what you have ('the sight of the eyes') rather than have roaming desires. But what a sorry state of affairs!

So the sage continues to point to sad realities, often contradicting time-honoured teachings which he finds too glib. He adds the comment that we should not expect things to change. A new person comes onto the scene—but underneath bears the same old name of 'Adam', frail man of the earth. He, like others, will not be able to get justice from those that are stronger than he.

All in all, the conclusion of this section is that with so many sad and disappointing things in life, it is hard to point to any profit in it all. It passes like a shadow, and who can say what achievement will remain when others follow on?

GUIDELINES

People are apt to explain life's difficulties rather confidently, as long as they have not yet experienced the force of them. Our sage had heard much said about the righteous prospering, about the satisfaction of a long life and a good burial, and children to continue the family line. He had even heard people speak glibly of God and dishonestly pledge him offerings. So in all our readings this week he was burning to tell it as it is, to face truth. But underlying that passion, surely, must be a faith in truth, a faith in the perplexing, mysterious reality we call 'God'.

A prisoner of the Gestapo, later to be hanged, Dietrich Bonhoeffer included some thoughts on Ecclesiastes in one of his letters:

We ought to find God and love him in the blessings he sends us… But everything in its season, and the important thing is to keep step with God, and not get a step or two in front of him (nor, for that matter, a step or two behind him, either).

'God seeketh again that which is passed away' (3:15)—this

means that God gathers up again with us our past which
belongs to us... Hence we ought not to seek the past again by
ourselves, but to do so with God.

Letters and Papers from Prison, SCM Press/Fontana, 1953, pages 56–57

Lord, abide with us,
for it is towards evening,
and the day is now far spent (see Luke 24:29).

7–13 OCTOBER   ECCLESIASTES 7–12

1   Mystery in the world and the heart *Read Ecclesiastes 7*

Eastern sages sometimes like to lead our thoughts by way of
contradicting our natural sentiments. After the first shock, you go
on reflecting and eventually may achieve a deeper wisdom. In this
fashion, our sage begins with several reversals of common feelings.
The opening melodious saying *tob shem mi-shemen tob*, 'a name is
more precious than precious ointment') is turned into a challenge
by the next line ('and the day of death, than the day of one's
birth'). This seems to mean that to die leaving a good name is a
happier event than a birth, with all the uncertainty still ahead. In
the background are the thoughts expressed earlier, that life can be
so unfair or futile that death seems preferable.

In a house where a death is mourned with fasting, the sage
continues, you may gain more wisdom about the human
condition than in a house where they are celebrating (perhaps a
birth) with feasting. Further, scolding words from a sage may be
more beneficial than the flattering tones of a fool.

After several more pieces of advice, the theme of chapter 3
recurs (v. 14). God has made contrasting experiences for us: in
some we should rejoice, and in the others reflect calmly, and
always with humility leave the outcome to him.

The recompense of righteousness and wickedness may seem
perverse (v. 15). Best not be too righteous or too wicked! The

teasing saying (vv. 16–17) is aimed against a self-destructive zealotry, and points to a wise moderation.

Examples are given of helpful wise counsels. It is good advice not to make too much of things you hear said against you (v. 21), and to beware of foolish sexual entanglements (v. 26). Yet how slight is the wisdom we can attain! The most famous of the wise tells us: 'I decided to become wise, but it was far from me. *That which is*, is far off and so deep, so deep' (vv. 23–24).

The human being itself is an immense puzzle. Our sage confesses he is baffled by the heart of men, still more by that of women (v. 28 may not be as misogynist as it sounds—'found' here may mean reaching a satisfactory understanding, as in v. 24 and 8:17). There is not a human being who is without sin (v. 20); God no doubt made the race simple and true, but they have looked for ever more devious ingenuities (v. 29).

2 'And therefore I praise joy' *Read Ecclesiastes 8*

A sage is not always sombre of countenance. When he tells the interpretation of some puzzling matter, his face lights up and his severe expression changes. Perhaps it was so with our sage, who now goes on to speak of service to the king or other powerful chief.

Heed what the king says, he advises, and the sacred duty of faithfulness. When you leave his presence, do not get involved in some mischief, for he holds sovereign power. You will not be able to say, 'Why are you acting so?' Carry out his command, and in wisdom judge the right moment.

Our sage reflects further that however careful we are, we cannot know what is to come. Just as we cannot control the wind, so we have no power over the day of our death. Just as there is no discharge when war is raging, so no device can give escape from death.

Reflecting more critically now on power (v. 9), he laments that one person should be able to mistreat another. He deplores also that such wealthy oppressors at death are taken from the city with solemn procession for burial, then back in the city their crimes are soon forgotten.

Divine retribution seems so slow to fall on the wicked that others are encouraged to do evil. Some sin a hundred times with impunity. In his heart the sage knows that goodness has its reward and neglect of God its penalty. But he regrets that it often appears that the dues of the righteous and the wicked have been switched around.

Struggling with the shortcomings of time-honoured wisdom and with the contradictions between the observing eye and the feeling heart, our sage concludes surprisingly, 'And therefore I praise joy.' Understanding is baffled, and the bright face of the wise teacher must darken again. But simple pleasures remain good gifts of God, and in these we must rejoice.

3   Seize the chance of life *Read Ecclesiastes 9*

The righteous and the wise, our sage concludes from much study of life, cannot determine their experiences. Love or hate may be their portion—it is all in the power of God. In any case, one fate will at last befall righteous and unrighteous alike, the fate of death.

The darkness deepens as he observes the advantage of the living: they know one thing for sure—that they will die. But the dead know nothing; their loves and hates are at an end, and they themselves become forgotten.

But again he recoils from total despair (vv. 7–9). He counsels enjoying all the opportunities of life—they are given with God's approval and favour. Along with the basic simplicities of work and daily food and drink, he mentions the wearing of white garments (as though every day was a special celebration) and he advises above all to enjoy life at the side of the beloved spouse. Life is indeed fleeting, but while the chance is there, do with all your strength whatever tasks God has put to your hand.

The joy is to be held onto in a perplexing world. Rewards do not necessarily go to those with ability, and no one can be safe from the net of calamity (vv. 11–12).

'There was once a little town'—here the sage begins a parable. A poor but wise man, by a skilful plan, saved the town from an invading army, but got no thanks and was soon forgotten. On another translation, he *would have* saved it, only they ignored him. Suiting this latter translation, the chapter ends (vv. 16–18) with reflections on what wisdom might achieve, especially for the peace of nations, if only it were heeded.

Here we have keen observations which each could foster much reflection. First, the fly in the ointment: a small speck of evil, yes only small, but see how it can ruin an otherwise good life! The heart of the wise inclines to the right hand, the positive, but the instinct of the foolish is to the left, the negative. The folly of the fool is obvious to everyone but himself. When the ruler loses his temper, hold your ground, and with a quiet spirit, relaxed and composed, you can overcome the crisis. Rewarding of merit often goes awry; the fools come out on top. Often a thrusting person rises from the bottom, while a truly noble soul is degraded.

Mishaps at work are to be expected (vv. 8–9). But perhaps these verses are metaphorical: aggressive acts rebound on the aggressor.

Like someone labouring with an unsharpened axe, so are all who act without wisdom. There is no reward for a bungled task, just as a snake-charmer will get no money—and may get worse, if the snake bites. The wise speak with simple grace; the foolish rave on without control. The fool multiplies words, although no one understands events or knows the future. How shy he is of work! And should he have to go out to a task, he gets too tired to find his way home!

Pity the country ruled by some ambitious servant surrounded by dissolute officials! Happy the land with a noble king, where feasting is held at its proper time! Roofing problems have always been with us, not least in Palestine where roofs were usually flat. They provide an illustration for the results of sloth—rotting rafters and a leaking roof.

People make bread for laughter and wine to gladden life—but for this and everything else they need to have the money. Reflection on this might turn to the need for ordered, diligent living, or to the sad fact that always some lack the basic necessities.

It is prudent not to curse the powerful, even in private. Things get about—through government spies or (if we take v. 20 literally) through the mystery of birds, which were reputed as messengers and tell-tales.

5 Light is sweet *Read Ecclesiastes 11*

The famous opening words have been read literally: send your grain overseas and in due course you will profit; but divide your goods, so that a disaster will not take them all. But it is hard to imagine that such grain export was significant in Jerusalem's life, and we may prefer the figurative understanding: give generously and widely, even when no return is in sight.

Two sayings emphasize our inability to control blessings or woes. Beyond our control, laden clouds shed the blessing of winter rain, and a great tree may fall this way or that.

Palestinian farmers faced some unpredictable weather. If you watch the wind and clouds too anxiously, says the sage, you may never sow or harvest. This may be meant more widely: do the good you can—if you wait for certainty of outcome, you will never act.

How mysteriously the life-spirit enters the bones of the child in the womb—and how far from our knowledge the secrets of the work of the God who makes all!

Early and late, a farmer works hard at sowing with no sure knowledge of success. So in all our days, early and late, we are to work at sowing good, not anxious for the result, which is in God's hand.

'The light is sweet...': here we have the essence of the counsel. Mindful of the long, long darkness that surrounds our life, we are to treasure every day of light and life. Let the young especially take the message to heart, for the prime of life is so soon gone. Let them take joy to their heart and eyes, yet keeping from the harmful ways displeasing to God.

6 Silver cord and golden bowl *Read Ecclesiastes 12*

Perhaps the secret of our sage is that his heart is truly that of a poet. He observes with a true and penetrating eye. He speaks of what he sees. Tragedy fills his lines, but also a love of light. And now, as he further counsels the young to be mindful of God and his good gifts while the life-force runs strong, he dwells with moving poetry on the ebbing of the beautiful gift of life. His long description of the fading of life's light in old age underlines his message that we should value and use life's opportunities while we have them.

Most precious is the phrase 'Remember thy Creator', for here our sage for once focuses the good and joyful life on awareness of God as our personal Lord and Maker. That good work the sage so often recommends flows from this—a life of daily creativity, responding to my Creator.

The weakening of the ageing body is then portrayed in poetic imagery. Bright sky succeeding heavy rain is not clear to aged eyes (v. 2). Hands, legs, teeth and eyes all fail (v. 3). Now is the time of the toothless mouth, restless nights, deafness (v. 4). The head is white, the limbs bent, desire gone, and the professional mourners already gather with an eye to employment (v. 5). They await that last out-breathing of life, when the breath returns to God who gave it.

The imagery here centres on the great symbols of light and water (vv. 6–7), which throughout the Bible are eloquent of the wonderful, beautiful divine gift of life. The light is imagined as from a bowl of oil in which a wick burns, the bowl suspended on a cord. The bowl is golden and the cord silver because the life they represent is so precious. The water is pictured as drawn from a deep well by the lowering of an earthenware vessel on a rope from a wheel. The final passing of life is expressed as the falling of the lamp from the broken cord, and the crash of the pitcher from the broken wheel. The light and the water are dashed out. The breath has returned to the Creator.

The concluding verses (9–14) are usually described as additions by editors. But perhaps we could imagine that our sage here puts aside his stage role of Solomon, Kohelet, the fabled collector of wise sayings, and adds the conclusion in his own person. He commends to us the preceding teachings as 'goads' and 'nails well fastened'. He warns against excessive hopes placed in books and their study (they are but the husks of wisdom, it was said in China). And he counsels again a life in humble awareness of God.

GUIDELINES

Cyprian Smith OSB, expounding a great medieval mystic, writes:

To say 'God' is to say that at the heart of the world we live in, the world of people and things, there lies an unfathomable mystery; when the scientists, philosophers, theologians and artists have said all the profound things they are able to say, there remains something unsaid—and unsayable. There is something refreshing about this fact. Great though Shakespeare, Newton and St Thomas Aquinas may be, it would be stifling and deadening if their sublime utterances contained the whole truth, if there were no reality beyond.

When St Thomas Aquinas, towards the end of his life, had a mystical glimpse of the true nature of God, it led him to see all his previous voluminous writings on theology as 'straw'; yet there is no hint that this was a depressing discovery for him. On the contrary it brought a sense of relief and joy. That which is holy must also be inviolate—something that cannot be debased by glib talk, cannot be controlled, abused, manipulated. To say that at the heart of the world lies a mystery is to glimpse the possibility that it may have some kind of ultimate meaning; that it may, after all, be worthwhile.

The Way of Paradox, DLT, London, 1987, pages 30–31

A recent presentation of Kohelet ends like this:

Even for this realistic philosopher, God is there at the end: 'and the breath returns to God who gave it'. He gave, he has taken back. Kohelet, your advice is good. I will remember him, live for him and from him all the days of my vigour. In him I will be content, and shall not fear when the lamp is broken, the leaves laid in the pit.

And when I embrace the gospel of the resurrection, I shall still be glad of the brave and sober foundation you have given. For all our hope is in the One we find, know and remember in this fleeting life.

John Eaton, Interpreted by Love, BRF, 1994, page 92

Help us, O Lord, to know the vanities of earthly life for what they are, and to find joy in your good gifts and life everlasting in you.

O Lord, support us all the day long of this troublous life, until the shades lengthen and the evening comes, and the busy world is hushed, the fever of life is over, and our work is done. Then, Lord, in thy mercy grant us safe lodging, a holy rest, and peace at the last; through Jesus Christ our Lord. Amen.

Further reading

R.N. Whybray, *Ecclesiastes: New Century Bible Commentary*, Eerdmann/Marshall, Morgan & Scott, Grand Rapids/London, 1989

Derek Kidner, *A Time to Mourn and a Time to Dance*, Inter-Varsity Press, Leicester, 1976

John Eaton, *The Contemplative Face of Old Testament Wisdom in the Context of World Religions*, SCM Press, London, 1989

The Gospel of Matthew—Part 2

In his first seven chapters, Matthew lays most of the foundations for the rest of his Gospel. Chapters 8 and 9 complete the job, with their depiction of Jesus the healer. Over the next four weeks, we shall see how Matthew emphasizes Jesus' authority as God's agent of salvation for Israel. Faith is the response he continually looks for—but what does this faith look like? The further we read, the clearer this becomes.

As the story progresses the disciples are increasingly drawn into Jesus' mission as agents and not merely spectators. We might expect their faith to be the strongest, but we repeatedly hear them referred to as 'you of little faith'. There is room for faith to grow—in us, as well as in them. But what does this faith develop into? The further we read, the more challenging this becomes, as Jesus and his followers face increasingly ominous opposition.

Some of the passages you are asked to read over the next four weeks are longer than others. This has proved to be inevitable if we are to reach the passion narrative in time for Lent next year.

These notes are based on the Revised Standard Version, though they can be used alongside any translation of the Bible.

14–20 OCTOBER   MATTHEW 8:1—10:42

---

1 **Authority and response: faith and service**
   Read Matthew 8:1–17

Matthew introduced the public ministry of Jesus in 4:23 by describing him as a teacher/preacher and healer. From a summary of the words of Jesus in the Sermon on the Mount, we move in chapters 8 and 9 to an outline of his healing actions, interspersed with briefer sections about discipleship. Matthew narrates ten of Jesus' mighty works (the number is perhaps intended as a reminder of the ten miracles Moses performed in Egypt—see Exodus 7–12). The stories are all found in Mark or Luke, though Matthew's are briefer. They emphasize the authority of Jesus, and highlight faith as the proper response to his healing work.

In these first three stories we see Jesus healing by various combinations of word and touch. The two men who encounter Jesus are on the edges of a religious system preoccupied with matters of purity. The leper's contagious skin disease excluded him from the temple, his family and his village (see Leviticus 13 and 14). As a local representative of the occupying imperial forces, the centurion was an outsider to Jewish society. Peter's mother-in-law's illness prevented her from fulfilling her household role. In all three stories we can see how illness is more than just a medical malfunction. Its social dimensions are just as significant as its biological ones—perhaps more so. Jesus makes it possible for the Jews he meets here to be reintegrated into society. And in his rare encounter with a Gentile, he shows that God's kingdom is wide open to anyone with faith.

This brings us to the characters' responses to Jesus. The leper and the centurion show great respect and call him 'Lord'. They both have enough faith to recognize his authority over illness. The centurion goes further. This broker of imperial favour comes to Jesus as the mediator of divine blessing. This representative of the all-conquering Caesar acknowledges the superior honour of Jesus. This figure whose commands issue in unquestioned obedience recognizes the supreme authority of Jesus' words—distance will not hinder their efficacy. Jesus is clearly impressed by the quality of this Gentile's faith. By contrast, no mention is made of the woman's faith—she does not ask to be healed, and the initiative lies entirely with Jesus. But her response is significant: Mark and Luke have her resuming her role in the household by serving 'them' (Mark 1:31; Luke 4:39). Matthew tells us that once she is recovered, she serves 'him'. The proper response to the healing power of God is a readiness to serve Jesus, whom Matthew identifies as the servant figure of Isaiah 53.

Note that Matthew considerably alters the sense of the Isaiah passage: unlike the earlier servant, Jesus is not directly affected by the diseases he heals. But there may be a hint here that the fulness of Jesus' healing work will only be achieved through his passion.

2 Where does faith lead? *Read Matthew 8:18–34*

Matthew often shows Jesus on the move. Here he cannot allow himself to be delayed in Capernaum, not even by the enormity of human need represented by the crowds. He has other priorities, which he expects his followers to share. He has to take his message and ministry elsewhere. This means that disciples— would-be and actual—must reckon with the cost of following this wandering charismatic figure. If people find themselves moved by Jesus' vision of salvation, they must be prepared to abandon the securities and comforts of home and family. They must even be ready to set aside the most sacred responsibilities to parents, so urgent are the priorities of God's coming kingdom. Launching out on the life of faith is not all plain sailing: it can be discomforting, demanding and even distressing.

The story of the stilling of the storm highlights this. Matthew's account is shorter than Mark's (4:36–41), and unlike Mark he has the disciples *following* Jesus into the boat. Matthew smoothes out the angularities of Mark's exchange between Jesus and his followers: here the disciples are told not to let their faith be swamped by fear. Rather, they are to trust Jesus, as one who mediates the power and authority of God. But where might such trust lead them? Will they always be protected from danger? The answers are found in the Gentile territory on the eastern shore of the sea.

Again Matthew's account is briefer than Mark's—though Matthew doubles the number of demoniacs, to bring out the authority of Jesus over the destructive power of evil. In a world which held that human beings could be influenced by invisible forces for good or ill, the bizarre behaviour of these frightening figures was taken as evidence that they were possessed by evil spirits. We might prefer to say that they had been 'driven mad'— but the difference in diagnosis should not obscure their plight. Condemned to live in a world of death among the tombs, they were outcasts in every sense. Jesus enabled them to return to their community, but the response he met only fulfilled his warning to the would-be disciple in verse 20. It is ironic that Jesus' single word to the demons is echoed in the locals' request that he leave their city.

Despite their escape on the sea, Matthew makes it clear that the disciples will not always be protected from the dangers of living in a destructive and divided world (as we shall see further in chapter 10). But they must not allow this to undermine their trust that in Jesus they are in touch with the power of God himself. Where does this faith lead in today's world?

3 The priority of mercy *Read Matthew 9:1–13*

Matthew continues to map out the authority of Jesus, now in his power to deal with sin (cf. 1:21). The two halves of this passage have a common pattern. First we are given Jesus' response to sin or sinners. Then we see how this provokes criticism from people who are concerned with the right interpretation of Jewish Law. Finally Jesus justifies his actions, and even claims divine authority for his scandalous behaviour.

Jesus' first words to the paralysed man reflect the traditional association of sin and sickness (see Deuteronomy 28:5ff.; Psalm 103:3), though elsewhere Jesus rejects these links (Luke 13:1–5). It would be no surprise if the man felt that his sins were responsible for his condition. Jesus' tender assurance provokes a hostile response from the scribes (interpreters of the Law). Notice the way Matthew sharpens the conflict between Jesus and his opponents, by describing their thoughts as 'evil'. Presumably they see Jesus as guilty of blasphemy because he ignores the God-given means of mediating forgiveness—the temple, its sacrifices and its priesthood. For his own part he claims to be acting as God's agent, the Son of man. According to popular belief (reflected in the parable in Matthew 25:31ff.), this figure would vindicate the righteous and condemn sinners at the last judgment. Jesus claims this authority for himself now, and demonstrates it by healing the paralysed man. Little wonder the crowds are amazed—the end of the world is dawning!

The controversy continues in Jesus' readiness to mix with undesirable individuals and classes. 'Matthew' (called Levi in the parallel accounts in Mark and Luke) would probably have worked for a man like Zacchaeus (Luke 19:1ff.). He would have been responsible for collecting taxes on produce, and tolls on services and goods passing through his district. He and his kind were despised by the educated rich and tradesmen—and by religious groups like the Pharisees, who put them in the same category as those they called 'sinners', and would not dream of eating with them. 'Sinners' were not so much moral failures as religious and social outcasts: they showed neither the ability nor the inclination to live by those parts of the Law that could be used to distinguish Jews from others. Zealous groups like the Pharisees believed it was important for the Jews in Palestine to maintain their distinctive identity, living as they did under the double occupation of imperial rule and foreign culture. Jesus subverts their social divisions, and justifies his behaviour by referring to popular wisdom. And he goes further by appealing to scripture (Hosea 6:6). When it is part of a divisive and oppressive system, animal sacrifice obscures the divine mercy that it is meant to symbolize, with disastrous consequences for human well-being.

In both these incidents, Jesus reasserts the priority of God's mercy, as we would expect from one who values it so highly (see 5:7; 6:12ff.; 7:1ff.). In verse 8 Matthew suggests that the power to declare this divine priority is not restricted to Jesus (cf. 10:8 and 18:18). What might this mean for the healing and reconciling work of the Church today?

4 Celebrating the breadth of new life Read Matthew 9:14–26

Verses 14–17 serve as a bridge between yesterday's reading and verses 18–26. They exhibit the familiar 'action-controversy-justification' pattern, but this time it is the behaviour of Jesus' disciples that causes offence. Their critics see fasting as a sign of mourning and protest in the face of evil. Jesus' remarks in verse 15 denounce such behaviour: it is as insulting to God as it would be to the host of a wedding feast. For the moment, celebration is a more appropriate sign of the appearance of God's kingdom. Mourning will have its day soon enough.

The sayings about the patch and the wineskins point forward to verses 18–26. Celebration not mourning is the order of the day because God's kingdom is first and foremost about life: it has a quality of newness and freshness that cannot be constrained by the old and inappropriate ways of interpreting the Law. Matthew uses the two healings to illustrate this. His account is ruthlessly pared to the bone, to highlight once again the importance of faith. Jesus does not allow the derision of the professional mourners to drown the father's faith: without uttering a word to the dead girl he fulfils the man's hopes. He heals the woman who interrupts his journey, even though her contact with him is fleeting, even superficial. The ruler and the woman represent different groups of people and they have different kinds of faith, yet they both have cause to celebrate because they fasten on to the same figure.

Jesus speaks only twice in this story, and his words reveal the breadth of the life he brings. The woman's illness would have made her unclean according to the canons of religious purity. Once a social and religious outcast, she could now resume her place in society as a true 'daughter' of Israel. The girl is dead, but in a sense she's only 'sleeping'. Her rising—like that of the paralysed man in 9:6–7—is a sign of the ultimate victory of God's reign of life over every kind of death (see Daniel 12:2; 1 Thessalonians 4:13). Even now that victory is making its mark on the world.

New wine needs new, not old, wineskins. The life that Jesus brings is not carried by religious systems that lead to fragmentation and separation, but by faith. The faith that draws people in all their diversity *to God* through Jesus Christ has the power to draw them *together*. Why is this far from being the normal Christian experience?

5 The range of responses to Jesus *Read Matthew 9:27–38*

We could be forgiven for thinking that these two healing stories are only included here to make up the number to ten (see on 8:1–17). Matthew has a fuller account of the healing of two blind men in 20:29–34, and the healing of a blind and dumb demoniac in 12:22–24 provokes a more extended counter-response from Jesus to those who cast aspersions about the source of his authority. Yet these two stories illustrate perfectly two extreme responses to Jesus, neither of which satisfies him.

Typically, Matthew highlights the importance of faith in the healing of the two blind men. But not for the first time in this Gospel (8:4; cf. 12:16) Jesus forbids any publicity. We may wonder why, when he seems only too pleased to welcome the great crowds who are often drawn to him. Perhaps the way the blind men address him provides a clue: 'Have mercy on us, *Son of David*'. Though there is no evidence that Jewish groups at the time expected the Messiah/Son of David to be a healer, the prophets had certainly hoped for a new world in which the sick would be healed (see Isaiah 29:18–19; 35:5–6; 61:1). It is possible that when these blind men (and others) saw the signs of newness appearing around Jesus, and heard him speaking about the coming of God's *kingdom*, they began to think of him as the kind of messianic figure who might lead a popular uprising against the Roman occupying forces. Jesus' ability to draw large crowds would only increase the risk of his being seen as a destabilizing agent. That would attract the wrong kind of publicity, and put an end to his mission.

As far as we know, the Pharisees had no particular political agenda. Their opposition to Jesus probably focused on his criticism of their way of preserving Israel's distinctive identity, which they believed was threatened by political and cultural occupation of their land. No doubt they recognized his subversive potential in the religious and social sphere. By accusing him of being in league with 'the prince of demons', they engage in the kind of name-calling that seeks to undermine his public credibility. Later in the Gospel we shall see how Jesus defends himself; for now we must be content with Matthew's observations on the risks attendant on Jesus' public ministry at a time of change and stress in Israel.

As well as popular acclaim and genuine faith, Jesus has to reckon with misunderstanding and opposition. But that doesn't diminish his compassion for the leaderless Galileans. He refuses to exploit their vulnerability for his own ends, such is his concern for them—so great, in fact, that he enlists the support of his closest disciples in extending his mission. Today's successors of those disciples are likely to encounter a range of responses to the gospel; they must allow nothing other than compassion to shape their approach to the wider world.

6 Sustaining the responsibilities of mission
Read Matthew 10:1–42

As in 4:23ff., the summary statement about Jesus' extensive ministry in 9:35ff. introduces another major block of teaching, this time on mission. Though Jesus mainly addresses the twelve disciples, by the end of the chapter he has others in mind— notably those who receive their ministry. Like the Sermon on the Mount, it is unlikely that Jesus presented this teaching on a single occasion. Comparison with Mark's and Luke's Gospels suggests that Matthew has shaped the discourse, to bring out not only the privileges and responsibilities of mission but also its demands and risks.

The list of the twelve disciples is much the same as in Mark 3:16ff. and Luke 6:14ff., though there are one or two differences. Only in Matthew are they told to restrict their ministry to Israel at this stage. Perhaps the twelve, then, are the nucleus of a renewed Israel, reconstituted by the coming of the kingdom of heaven in Jesus' ministry. Jesus authorizes the twelve to extend the work he has been doing (vv. 7–8, 26–27). They are to travel light and rely on people's generosity. They are to have a sense of urgency and boldness, and dissociate themselves from those who withhold hospitality (which was at the heart of the crimes of Sodom and Gomorrah in Genesis 19). A healthy realism will serve them well: the house of Israel is not only like a cornfield ready for harvest, it is also land on which sheep graze. The agents of Jesus' mission are not just workers who bring home the harvest; they are also vulnerable to attack by unscrupulous predators.

Verses 17–22 have parallels in Mark 13:9ff. and Luke 21:12ff., though they are missing from the corresponding section of Matthew 24. Has Matthew brought them forward to this point in his Gospel in order to highlight the risks and dangers of the disciples' mission? Though the details reflect the later experience of the Church, the evangelist is surely right to have Jesus remind his followers of the down-side of mission from the outset (cf. 5:11–12). As disciples and servants, their way of life is bound up with that of their teacher and master. Like him they must set aside all other loyalties, even kinship. Unlike the impression given by the story in 8:23–27, Jesus makes no promises about guarding them from danger. So what will sustain them in their mission, if they cannot rely on family support or divine protection? Dependence on the Holy Spirit, trust in God's care for them, confidence that God will in the end vindicate them and their cause—these are the dimensions of the faith that will enable them to weather the storms that lie ahead.

GUIDELINES

Jesus' words to the disciples about mission are full of paradox. He empowers the agents of his mission, but clearly they are also vulnerable ('sheep in the midst of wolves') and weak ('little ones'). He tells them to overcome the divisions in Israel, but suggests that their work, like his, will create division not peace. There are no assured results in the work of God's kingdom, no marketing strategy that will guarantee success. There is only the privilege of representing Jesus and the One who sent him. In the end, this is reward enough—for them and for us.

21–27 OCTOBER   MATTHEW 11:1—13:52

---

1   Agents of wisdom: comparisons and contrasts
     Read Matthew 11:1–19

As Jesus resumes his itinerant ministry, Matthew wants his readers to be in no doubt that he is indeed Israel's Messiah. But not everyone shares the evangelist's opinion—notably John the Baptist, languishing in Herod's prison (4:12; 14:3ff.). Perhaps the style and scope of Jesus' ministry have surprised John: the one whom he baptized doesn't fit any of the traditional expectations of Spirit-anointed leadership. Or does he? Jesus' response to the Baptist's disciples directs them to the evidence of their eyes and ears. If they will only set his words and works against the ancient hopes for Israel's renewal expressed by the prophets, they will find the answer to their question (see Isaiah 29:18–19; 35:5–6; 61:1). Can they not see that Israel's longings for a new world are at last being fulfilled?

The Baptist's enquiry gives Jesus the opportunity to broadcast his opinion of him. Jesus clearly has a high regard for John. He admires his unflinching approach, and his determination to highlight Israel's plight from the margins of society rather than compromise with the powerful élites of cities like Jerusalem. John may have his doubts about Jesus, but Jesus is utterly convinced of the significance of John. Imprisoned he may be, but this is no self-appointed critic of the establishment. He is the last and greatest of Israel's prophets, the expected Elijah who will prepare Israel for the day of God's coming (Malachi 3:1ff.). Yet for all this, the Baptist concludes a chapter of Israel's history that has now finished. By contrast the Messiah opens a new, more glorious one.

Verse 12 is not easy to understand, and in the corresponding passage of Luke it reads very differently (Luke 7:16). The alternative translations (see the footnotes in the text) raise the question as to whether the kingdom is the object or the subject of violence. The answer may well come from the experience of its leading lights—the imprisoned John, the bridegroom Jesus who will one day be taken away, and the sheep-like disciples. To borrow the imagery of an earlier story, it is not all plain sailing for the kingdom of heaven. Those who take up its cause must reckon with the likelihood of a rough ride.

From John the Baptist, Jesus turns his attention to those of his contemporaries who rejected them both. Perhaps the fickleness of their responses is an indication of the seriousness of the challenge John and Jesus present to the status quo. Their strategies may have been different, but John and Jesus are both in some measure agents of God's wisdom. Jesus suggests that the value of their respective ministries is not measured by their ability to drum up popular support, but by the integrity and outcome of their deeds. This is something the Church in every age needs to remember.

2 Shaping the response to God's revelation
Read Matthew 11:20–30

We have seen how the progress of the Gospel narrative has been marked by increasingly polarized responses to Jesus. Now we are told that three whole communities have rejected him. Chorazin, Bethsaida and Capernaum are prosperous settlements around the northern shores of the Sea of Galilee: did Jesus' teaching offend their inhabitants' comfortable lifestyles? Startlingly, these Jewish cities (their populations were small by modern standards) are compared unfavourably with the stereotypical centres of resistance to God in the scriptures. The Mediterranean coastal towns of Tyre and Sidon were sometimes condemned by the prophets (see Isaiah 23; Ezekiel 26), and Sodom has had a bad press ever since Genesis 18 and 19.

Such widespread rejection of Jesus, particularly by the powerful élites from the cities, might call his status into question. Is the future that Israel has been looking forward to for centuries actually beginning to take shape in this man's words and works, as he claims? Does he really have the authority to define the texture of Israel's response to God, as he maintains? With the build-up of opposition and rejection, verses 25–30 underline the authority and significance of Jesus in the face of all that undermines them.

Human response to Jesus depends ultimately on God, who reveals his will and purpose not to the 'wise and understanding' (the powerful) but to 'babes'—those who live as Jesus does, out of dependence and trust in God. But this does not mean that God discriminates in favour of some rather than others; it is more a case of earthly power and status getting in the way of all that God discloses in Jesus. Verse 27 is a proverbial Jewish expression of the relationship between fathers and sons: try reading it without the capital letters adopted by most translations (the effect of interpreting it in the light of the Fourth Gospel). As sons are dependent on, and important to, their fathers, so it is with Jesus and the heavenly Father. He can therefore speak with supreme authority in the disputes over the nature of Israel's salvation.

Verses 28–30 draw together the threads of Jesus' teaching, and echo the Beatitudes in 5:3ff. Peasant farmers would readily grasp the significance of the yoke as an image of the controlling influence on a person's life. Jesus issues an invitation to allow *his* way and character to shape and direct the human response to God. His yoke is easy and light because it liberates people from anxiety and self-concern, and enables them to live according to the Sermon on the Mount—trustfully, mercifully, generously. What difference might it make to you, and the people around you, if you tried to live more of this week according to these words of Jesus?

3 Who speaks and acts for God? *Read Matthew 12:1–30*

As opposition to Jesus builds up, Matthew now concentrates on those whom he sees as its major orchestrators, the Pharisees. In three incidents here he picks up the threads of the earlier story in 9:32ff., to set out two main areas of dispute: the sabbath and the source of Jesus' authority.

At the time of Jesus, sabbath observance meant more than Israel's remembering her dependence on God the creator (Exodus 20:8). Like circumcision and the laws relating to food, it had become part of Israel's purity code, and therefore a means of identifying genuine members of Israel. The more zealous among the Pharisees (and other groups like the Essenes) see plucking and rubbing heads of grain, and even healing, as unnecessary work, and therefore taboo, on the sabbath. Jesus disagrees: there are biblical precedents (vv. 3–5) and contemporary practices (v. 11: some, though not all, Pharisees would help a stranded animal on the sabbath; among the Essenes this was explicitly forbidden) which show that sustaining life is more important than preserving sectarian purity. This has to be the case when mercy is the paramount expression of God's will (cf. 9:13).

How does Jesus fulfil Isaiah's reference to the Gentiles at this stage of the narrative, especially after 10:6 and in anticipation of 15:24? There are echoes of Jesus' baptism in the passage (cf. 3:16–17). Then as now, he is said to be endowed with the Spirit of God and therefore able to act with divine authority as God's servant. And the scope of the servant's mission shows that God's interests are not restricted to the nation of Israel. Matthew wants to show that those who criticize Jesus for contravening separatist purity regulations are out of step with God.

This brings us to the deeper issue behind these criticisms of Jesus. Who has the right to speak for God in Israel, to define the shape of his salvation, to give conclusive expression to his will: those who promote 'the politics of holiness' (as the system founded on separatist purity has been called), or Jesus? By accusing Jesus of being in league with the powers of evil, his opponents hope to shame him publicly and thus undermine his public credibility—in other words, to destroy him (v. 14). Matthew's readers know that the Pharisees' suggestion in verse

24 is ludicrous: Jesus was conceived by the Spirit, endowed with the Spirit in his baptism, and led by the Spirit into the wilderness, where he defeated Satan. But his critics need to realize the absurdity of their charge. Satan's kingdom clearly has not yet fallen, as the work of the Pharisees' own exorcists shows—or are they too in league with Beelzebul? In verse 29 Jesus uses an evocative parable to picture his Spirit-endowed work as the agent of God's kingdom. Does this suggest that he is now returning the strong man's goods to their rightful owner (i.e. God)? Do these goods include the Jewish Law, which is abused when it becomes the vehicle of sectarianism? Is Jesus now freeing the Law for its rightful use? If this really is what he is claiming, we can understand why he provokes such opposition, and why his ministry leaves no space for any middle ground (v. 30).

4 What drives the opponents of Jesus? *Read Matthew 12:31–50*

The exchange between Jesus and his opponents intensifies as he warns them about the seriousness of their attitudes towards him. The saying about the sin against the Holy Spirit has troubled many readers of the Gospels. Wherever it occurs (Mark 3:29; Luke 12:10), the context is conflict rather than the quest to discover the truth about Jesus. His opponents here are not struggling to understanding him—then mistakes would be inevitable, as in any genuine learning process. Rather, they are wilfully misrepresenting him (just as the false prophets of 7:16–20 misrepresent God). Their insults provide unmistakable evidence of the evil in their hearts. Accusing someone of being evil today might be an attempt to short-circuit the demanding business of trying to comprehend why they act or speak as they do. But Jesus discerns only too well what lies behind this particular conflict: his opponents have lost the ability to distinguish between good and evil. Is this because they are hell-bent on promoting their own place in society and securing their own stake in Israel's coming salvation? Their poisonous desire for power and honour will prove eternally damaging.

The request for a sign to validate Jesus' authority claims is entirely understandable. But his response only amplifies his earlier accusation about the real motives of his opponents: not only are they evil, they are also unfaithful to God. In Jesus' day adultery involved one man taking (or even desiring—see 5:28) another man's property (his wife) and treating her as if she were his own. These scribes and Pharisees are guilty of taking what belongs to God (that is, Israel and the Law) and using it for their own ends. The stark, uncompromising dualism of Jesus' language invites his opponents to do some serious heart-searching and repent. His biblical examples show that even Gentiles are capable of embracing less worthy representatives of God than him—which suggests that these Pharisees have no excuse for continuing to resist Jesus' call.

Repentance must be whole-hearted, though. It is no use emptying the house of evil without filling it with good. True repentance involves the whole person—heart and mind, attitudes and motivation—in a radical response to Jesus' vision of the kingdom of heaven. Nothing less will do, because Jesus disconnects the traditional links between nation, family and salvation which allow misguided assumptions and evil actions to flourish. At the heart of God's kingdom lies a new reality, a different kind of kinship, in which doing the will of God as understood by Jesus makes people into brothers and sisters, mothers and fathers. The whole tenor of Jesus' words here suggests that to endanger this project of redemption is to court evil.

5 Broadcasting the gospel Read Matthew 13:1–23

The seven parables of chapter 13 constitute the third main block of Jesus' teaching in this Gospel. Four of the stories are found in the corresponding sections of Mark (chapter 4) and Luke (chapter 8), and three are not found elsewhere. As in the other collections of Jesus' teaching, Matthew's hand is evident here too, not least in the way he uses this section to comment on the story of his Gospel so far. Since Jesus began his public ministry in chapter 4, we have seen a variety of responses to his ministry, and as the story has progressed hostility and opposition to Jesus have only increased. What has been happening as the gospel has been broadcast throughout Galilee?

The parable of the sower interprets the various responses to Jesus through the commonplace events of agricultural life. Jesus the preacher and teacher is like the peasant farmer scattering seed over his fields. Just as different kinds of soil produce different amounts of growth, so people's responses vary to the word of the kingdom. The parable and its interpretation invite us to look back over the Gospel: the response from the path corresponds to the Jewish leaders; the rocky ground reminds us of the threats to the disciples' 'little faith' (8:23–27); the thorny ground recalls Jesus' warning in 6:24; and the good soil produces all that Jesus and Matthew are looking for. By attaching the parable of the feuding farmers (more commonly known as 'the parable of the tares') to that of the sower, Matthew highlights once again the conflict that Jesus provokes (see the next section of notes for further discussion of this parable and its explanation).

Matthew includes more than Mark or Luke on Jesus' conversation with the disciples about his reasons for speaking in parables. Unlike the crowds, his closest followers are particularly privileged: verses 11–12 and 16–17 echo 11:25. The parables have the same effect as the words of the prophets, not least because Jesus demands something from his hearers. He does not present his message 'on a plate': there are no easily digestible 'sound bites' designed for ready consumption. By telling stories Jesus invites the crowds to allow the word of God's kingdom to enter their world and challenge them. But if they are not prepared to 'perceive... hear... and understand' what he has to say to them, then they will lose the relatively little (v. 12) that comes their way.

What do you find most challenging about the parable of the sower?

6 Words of encouragement and warning
Read Matthew 13:24–52

In the first of the seven parables we saw how Jesus' preaching was compared to the everyday action of the peasant farmer. The remaining six make the comparisons between the coming of the kingdom of heaven and everyday life even more explicit, and contain words of encouragement and warning. So the conflict between Jesus and his opponents is compared to feuds in which one family seeks to undermine the honour of another. The growth of the mustard seed illustrates well the contrast between the small scale of the kingdom in the present and what it will become in the future. The use of yeast shows how something that is easily hidden can have great power to effect change. The consequence of finding treasure and pearls illustrates the enormous value of the kingdom to those who discover its secrets. And the net full of all sorts of fish warns against expecting clear demarcations between good and evil in the present-day work of the kingdom.

In Mark and Luke, only one parable—the sower—is explained. In verses 37–43 Jesus continues the term-for-term approach found in verses 18–23, to explain the parable of the feuding farmers. Many biblical scholars consider the more likely source of these interpretations to be the evangelist rather than Jesus. One reason for this is that verses 37–43 contain some characteristic Matthean themes, such as the Son of man as the agent of the last judgment, and the final separation of good and evil (see 25:31ff., and compare vv. 49–50, both of which are only in Matthew). By addressing them to the disciples rather than the crowds, Matthew applies the details of Jesus' teaching to the situations his readers were facing.

In these parables of judgment and separation the accent falls on what will happen in the future, at 'the close of the age' when the kingdom of heaven comes in all its fulness and the righteous enter their glorious destiny (compare v. 43 with Daniel 12:1). But they also have a bearing on the present, particularly for those who claim to understand his teaching and interpret it correctly to others (vv. 51–52). The 'treasure' of these disciple-scribes is their dedication to God (6:21; cf. v. 44), from which they claim to draw everything in their lives (this seems to be the sense of 'what is new and what is old' in v. 52). But those who think of themselves as righteous must be on their guard in case they become agents of evil.

GUIDELINES

There is much in Jesus' parables for today's communicators of the gospel to consider. Here are a few suggestions.

- *It is important that we too use stories that invite people to respond to Jesus, rather than confront them with commands or threats. But we must broadcast the gospel without trivializing its message.*

- *We should not underestimate the many hindrances to the growth of the gospel seed. There is no room for unrealistic expectations about progress and success.*

- *The attempt to establish clear demarcations between good and evil, insiders and outsiders is a misuse of time and energy.*

- *While it is encouraging to know that there will always be a harvest, we also have to reckon with waste: some of our efforts simply do not bear fruit. Commending the gospel in the real world demands patience, as well as wisdom and courage.*

---

28 OCTOBER–3 NOVEMBER   Matthew 13:53—17:8

1   An offensive and threatening prophet
Read Matthew 13:53—14:12

The seed continues to fall on stony ground as Jesus returns to his home territory. The references to his family remind us of 12:46ff. There Jesus undermined the conventional wisdom on the importance of family ties in his rather shocking statement that kinship no longer has its traditional priority. Here his opponents show how far they are from his vision of God's kingdom by allowing family ties to dictate their attitudes towards him. Familiarity breeds contempt—and this acts as a stumbling block for the possibility of faith.

Herod the tetrarch (one of the sons of the now dead Herod the Great, whom we met in chapter 2) supplies an answer to the question posed in verse 54. Like John, Jesus too is a prophet—so he gets his power from God. Does this mean that Herod finds Jesus' fame just as threatening as John's? John had offended Herod by criticizing his marriage to Herodias as contrary to Jewish Law, because her husband Philip was still alive. According to the Jewish historian Josephus, Herod acted against John because his popular appeal made him a destabilizing influence. As a puppet king charged with keeping the peace in the territories delegated to him, Herod could hardly afford to upset his imperial overlords. Josephus may offer the more plausible reason for John's arrest and execution, but these alternative explanations are not entirely incompatible. By arresting and executing John, Herod effectively silenced the criticism from this popular prophet.

Herod's treatment of John reveals the flaws in his own character. But more important for the Gospel narrative is this instance of the clash between prophets and powerful rulers. Verses 12 and 13 strongly suggest that John's fate anticipates Jesus'. For different reasons, Jesus' ministry also endangers the delicate balance of power in a nation under imperial occupation. As Jesus draws nearer to Jerusalem, his Galilean opponents will give way to the powerful vested interests associated with the temple. For the moment Jesus evades Herod's attention by withdrawing from public view. But Matthew leaves us in no doubt where the conflict surrounding Jesus is leading.

2 The unlimited compassion of the Son of God
   Read Matthew 14:13–36

Reports of Jesus' healing ministry in verses 14 and 35 bracket three unusual stories, two of which are found in all four Gospels (though with significant differences), with one unique to Matthew. The feeding of a crowd in excess of 5,000 people (only Matthew refers to the women and children) has echoes in the Jewish scriptures, the last meal that Jesus shared with his disciples, and the eucharistic life of the early Church. Moses fed a large crowd in the wilderness (see Exodus 16 and Numbers 11). Elisha fed a hundred men with twenty loaves of barley and some grain, and had food to spare (2 Kings 4:42–44). Deuteronomy 18:15, 18 anticipates the appearance of a 'prophet like Moses', and there is evidence that some Jews expected the Messiah to repeat the manna miracle. So the feeding story presents Jesus as the prophet-Messiah who fulfils the ancient hopes of Israel. He nourishes and sustains God's people by giving up his own life for them. He makes the fruits of his generosity readily available to those who 'do this in remembrance' of him.

Jesus eventually achieves the solitude he desires by dismissing both crowds and disciples. While he prays, his followers struggle to make headway in the boat. We are reminded of the earlier story in 8:23–27: this time physical distance rather than sleep renders Jesus inaccessible. Or does it, because distance is seen to be no obstacle to the exercise of his compassion? What are we to make of Jesus' walking on the water? Margaret Davies notes the parallels between Jesus walking over the sea before daybreak and the Holy Spirit moving over the waters before the creation of light (Genesis 1:2). The Church struggling against all kinds of waves and wind can be full of faith rather than doubt or fear, because in Jesus it has access to the creative energies of God.

Matthew highlights the call to faith by inserting the story of Peter's walking on the water between Jesus' words to the disciples in verse 27 (cf. Mark 6:50) and the wind ceasing in verse 32 (cf. Mark 6:51). Peter starts to sink under the weight of his own uncertainty, as he will do when he denies Jesus before the crucifixion. The power of Jesus to rescue him evokes a positive response from the rest of the disciples (contrast Mark). They echo the heavenly voice which addresses the Spirit-anointed Jesus after his baptism (3:17), and anticipate the centurion's confession at the cross (27:54).

We can see something of the genius of Matthew in this passage. Having made it abundantly clear that Jesus' conflict with the authorities will bring about his execution, he now insists that Jesus' death will not diminish his saving power. Whenever people gather together to worship the Son of God by taking, blessing, breaking and distributing bread, it is as if they are among the crowds in the lonely place or with the disciples on the boat. Their hunger will be satisfied, their fears and doubts will be stilled, as they exercise faith in the unlimited compassion of the Son of God.

3 The most destructive kind of defilement *Read Matthew 15:1–20*

Pharisees and their scribes have questioned, challenged, accused and generally impugned the honour of Jesus from chapter 9 onwards. Here, for the first time, Matthew mentions connections between Jesus' opponents and Jerusalem. It may be that these particular Pharisees and scribes were closely associated with the temple, the symbolic centre of Judaism. The temple's architecture embodied the purity system, with its separation of clean and unclean (Jew from Gentile, male from female, priest from people). The point at issue in this exchange is a vivid example of the operation of that system. Washing the hands before eating here is not a matter of hygiene but of ritual purity, showing one's separation from a world that is believed to be unclean.

Jesus' immediate response makes no reference to ritual washing. Instead he deals with the more general issue of hypocrisy. In their attempt to live by the Torah, these Pharisees and scribes are said to regulate their conduct by 'the traditions of the elders', particular applications of the Law preserved largely in oral tradition. Jesus maintains that these traditions can quench the spirit of the Law. As an example, he refers to the dedication of money to God rather than using it to support parents. It is not clear whether he has in mind actual gifts to the temple or oaths that merely promise a sum of money. Either way, these fiscal practices enhance the standing of the donor at the expense of allowing parents to receive the honour due to them (note Jesus' positive attitude to the family on this occasion). The central thrust of the Torah—love for God demonstrated in love of neighbour— is thereby nullified, and those who claim to put God and others first are exposed as hypocrites whose primary interest lies in their own honour.

For Jesus, what comes out of the heart is more important than what goes into the stomach (food was another key indicator of ritual purity). Purity of heart (5:8) is what matters, rather than dividing the world into clean and unclean, insiders and outsiders. The examples of moral defilement in verse 19 are associated with violence and social disorder. Ironically these are always the ultimate consequence of pursuing ritual purity. Separatism of whatever kind, however it is justified, ultimately proves to be destructive.

Once again the image of the Pharisees and their scribes is badly tarnished. Reading Matthew's Gospel at a distance from the actual circumstances, both of Jesus' ministry and the church(es) for whom he was writing, can lead to a dangerous stereotyping of all Pharisees, and indeed all Jews, as evil. So we must read with care, always alert to the fact that we can all fall into the trap of making void the word of God through hypocrisy.

4 Crossing boundaries with faith and compassion
Read Matthew 15:21–39

Jesus has been trying to escape from the crowds since 14:13. We now find him in Syria, well away from Jewish territory, in the region around the Mediterranean ports of Tyre and Sidon. His encounter with the Gentile woman continues the theme of yesterday's reading, though his initial response to her contains echoes of the separatist sentiments repudiated there.

Comparison with Mark's version of this encounter (Mark 7:24–30) reveals an identical basic storyline. But for once Matthew breaks with his habitual brevity: verses 22–26 are significantly longer than their Markan equivalent. Matthew refers to the woman as a 'Canaanite' rather than 'a Greek, a Syrophoenician by birth' as in Mark. 'Canaanite' is a biblical as well as racial term: here she is not merely a Gentile, but a representative of an idolatrous people. Jesus' silence, the disciples' demands that he send her away, and his remark about the restriction of his mission to the Jews conspire to distance him from her. Where Matthew returns to his habit, his brevity only increases that distance. 'Let the children first be fed' (Mark 7:27) hints, however slightly, at the possibility that the dogs might expect at least something. But here the dogs (a Jewish term of abuse for Gentiles) can expect nothing.

By exploiting the distance between Jesus and the Canaanite woman, Matthew succeeds in highlighting the quality of her faith. We are on familiar ground here: reminders of previous encounters with Gentiles and Jews abound (see 8:10; 9:22, 27ff.). The woman exemplifies perfectly the attitude Jesus looks for in his first Beatitude (5:3), and her blessing is confirmed in the immediate granting of her request (cf. 8:13).

Jesus is apparently still in Gentile territory in verses 29–39 (v. 39 suggests that he has to cross from the east side of the sea to reach Jewish territory once more on the west bank). There is nothing new in crowds flocking to him to be healed—except that Matthew twice singles out 'the lame, the maimed and the blind'. The Essenes specifically excluded these categories of Jews from any hope of being included among God's covenant people. Here these doubly-excluded, handicapped Gentiles end up praising 'the God of Israel'. But this is a different 'Israel' from the one envisaged by Jesus' opponents, with their separatist deity. The second feeding story only underlines this. Numbers apart (echoes of the four corners of the earth and the seven Gentile nations give the meal an international flavour), it is identical to the earlier one in 14:13ff. In both cases, Jesus' compassion lies behind his blessing the hungry—it matters not whether they are Gentiles or Jews.

Faith and compassion—not for the first time does Matthew remind us of their power to cross the most intractable human boundaries. What boundaries might they have to cross today? How far do they take you with them?

5   Interpreting the signs of the time *Read Matthew 16:1–20*

Matthew increases the dramatic tension in his narrative by replaying the earlier demand for a sign in 12:38ff. With all that has happened since then, it comes as no surprise that these Pharisees and Sadducees, as representatives of official Judaism (the Sadducees were the aristocratic families from whom the temple priesthood were drawn), should repeat their insistence that Jesus authorize his actions.

Matthew has a low opinion of Jesus' opponents: like Satan in 4:1, they come to 'test' him. Jesus' disciples cannot afford to allow their impressions of him to be moulded by the increasing intensity of opposition. Their powers of perception must be razor-sharp if they are to see the signs of God's kingdom in the face of growing official disquiet. The disciples reveal their dullness by failing to grasp Jesus' riddle about the leaven. They think he is talking about their shortage of bread, but he is more concerned about their lack of insight. By now they ought to realize that the leaven of the kingdom (13:33) has its counterpart in the leaven of evil—which includes his opponents' power to manipulate public opinion about Jesus and his cause.

So for the first time Jesus probes the depth of his disciples' 'little faith' by asking them a direct question. How aware are they of the opinions of others? How much are they influenced by them? We already know that Herod sees Jesus as John the Baptist, whom Jesus identified with Elijah (11:14). Elijah also had a habit of upsetting Israel's rulers. The rejected and persecuted Jeremiah could be a fierce critic of the temple. Does Jesus fit somewhere into this hierarchy of Israel's prophets? Peter's answer is more fulsome than in Mark 8:29 or Luke 9:20, and the extra words in his confession echo 3:17—4:11. Despite his difficulty with the riddle of the leaven, Peter can after all make sense of 'the signs of the time'. Divine revelation has illuminated his 'little faith' (11:25; 13:11), and he proves to be a true prophet (does 'Bar-Jona' mean that he is a 'son of Jonah' the prophet?). Jesus goes on to identify himself with the wise man in his own parable (7:24ff.), by promising to build his house on the rock of Peter's confession. That house is the Church (only in Matthew does Jesus refer to the Church, here and at 18:17), the new community of Israel brought into being by the Messiah.

In verse 19 Jesus maintains that his house will have the authority to represent heaven on earth. How does the Church live up to this astonishingly high calling? In the light of Matthew's understanding of faith in 7:24ff., correct doctrine or church order are not enough. Only foundations that are sunk deep into the rock of Jesus' words and deeds will ensure that it survives the storms and floods of destruction and death.

6 Vocation and vindication *Read Matthew 16:21—17:8*

Jesus' command to silence in verse 20 seems unusual after his effusive response to Peter's confession. But now that his disciples can place him in the scheme of God's purposes, it is vital that they know how he will carry out his mission. He expects to meet a similar fate to those with whom he is compared (v. 14). Indeed he sees it as his vocation—what he *must* do—to face suffering, rejection and death from powerful Jewish leaders associated with the temple in Jerusalem. So far he has had no dealings with them in this Gospel, though his opponents in Galilee have sometimes had links with Jerusalem. Opposition, though, is not confined to opponents: disciples can also become obstacles. Like the

Pharisees and Sadducees who test Jesus in 16:1, Peter comes to represent 'Satan'. The rock will become a stumbling block if Peter tries to make the Messiah in his own image.

Earlier in the Gospel Jesus warned would-be followers that his way is far from easy. He now picks up some earlier words from 10:38–39, to impress upon his hearers that his own vocation is to be the pattern for theirs. Discipleship has no room for natural inclinations towards self-preservation, involving as they so often do the desire to meet violence with violence. Disciples are to have their centre of gravity outside themselves, in the Messiah Jesus and his cause—just as he centres his life on the will of God and the kingdom of heaven. Far from being a recipe for instability and disaster, the messianic pattern will enable them to share in the destiny God has in store for his people. According to verse 27, Jesus' messianic way is the standard against which their lives will be judged.

Jesus Messiah lives out his own teaching, but still his hard words cry out for vindication. The enigmatic verse 28 (which appears in a slightly different form in Mark 9:1 and Luke 9:27) suggests that it will soon come, within a generation—or perhaps within a week for those who accompany him onto the mountain. The curious experience of the transfiguration is intended to convince these uncertain disciples that Jesus' way of being Messiah is backed by the highest possible authority. He is like Elijah and Moses, rejected by God's people but supported by God. Compared with the versions in Mark and Luke, Matthew's account heightens the heavenly dimensions of the vision: Jesus' face (like that of Moses in Exodus 34:29) shines, his clothes are white as light and the disciples are moved to worship. The heavenly voice echoes perfectly the words at Jesus' baptism, thereby endorsing all that he has been saying about his vocation. However difficult it is for the disciples to grasp Jesus' disturbingly unexpected way of being Messiah, they are to 'listen to him', and let his closing words of reassurance take them down the mountain and back to the fray.

Mercy, purity of heart, the refusal to meet violence with violence—these are among the features of the faith Jesus looks for in this week's readings. Faith like this is the hallmark of the messianic way, for Jesus as well as his followers. It can never be enough for us merely to say the Creed or think that 'Jesus is Lord'. Christianity is not just a means towards inner peace in an increasingly stressful world. Faith is a way of living that weaves together mind, will and heart, thoughts, words and deeds into a seamless whole. The substance and measure of this faith is Jesus himself: he is the rock on which the life he advocates is built. To say with Peter, 'You are the Christ, the Son of the living God' is to measure faith by conformity with the messianic way, even when that leads to 'Jerusalem'.

4–10 NOVEMBER   MATTHEW 17:9—20:34

1   Necessary and unnecessary offensiveness
   Read Matthew 17:9–27

The announcement of Jesus' messianic suffering in the last section is reinforced here as the narrative is punctuated by two further references to his passion. For now the disciples are to say nothing about their mountain-top experience. It is more important that they recognize that the lives of the Messiah and his forerunner—'Elijah, who is to restore all things' (Malachi 4:5)—are stamped with the same die. Anger at the first announcement of Jesus' passion (16:22) gives way to anxiety in verse 23. The disciples do not want to lose their Master, not least because in his absence their faith is woefully inadequate.

This comes out in the father's complaint about the disciples' inability to heal his 'moonstruck' (the literal meaning of the word translated as 'epileptic' in v. 15) son, despite the fact that Jesus has given them authority to heal (10:1). Jesus' disappointment and frustration are evident in verse 17, and the contrast between his faith and theirs is apparent in the boy's instantaneous cure once Jesus takes over. Throughout the Gospel their 'little faith' has made it hard for them to understand or trust Jesus (see 6:30; 8:26; 14:31; 16:8). Here it renders them powerless in the face of the destructiveness that threatens the boy. Their faith needs to grow and develop, as the comparison with the mustard seed suggests. A more robust spiritual discipline would surely help (note that v. 21 is not in the best manuscripts—it seems to have been added from Mark 9:29).

At first sight the story of the temple tax doesn't follow on easily from these discussions about messianic suffering and faith. Not all Jews paid the annual half-shekel towards the upkeep of the temple, despite Exodus 30:13—for example, the Essenes refused to contribute to an institution they considered to be corrupt. Jesus was prepared to pay, but not out of obligation. He reserved the right for himself and his followers—as sons of the heavenly Father, the supreme king—not to support the temple. But he exercised his freedom by paying the tax rather than causing offence. Coming at the end of a section in which Jesus' remarks have offended and disturbed his closest followers, this incident encourages us to distinguish between necessary and unnecessary offensiveness. Matthew's communities would find ample food for thought here as they considered their relations with the synagogue. There is a world of difference between the offensiveness of the messianic vocation and the deliberate provocation of another religious community. One is motivated by genuine faith and arises out of true devotion to God—the other is just another form of violence.

2 The messianic way to estimate honour *Read Matthew 18:1–14*

As Matthew's narrative has unfolded the nature of faith has been developing. At its heart is the element of openness to Jesus. True faith means hearing his words and acting on them; living out of trust in the providence of God and the benevolence of Jesus the healer; putting God's care to the test in the face of conflicting priorities, disappointment and even rejection. From 16:13 onwards, Matthew has begun to focus on what it means to be open to the messianic way of Jesus, with his talk of rejection and execution. His vision of God's kingdom is at odds with popular expectations, and their associated images of greatness and power.

So in the first part of the fourth of Jesus' discourses, Matthew addresses some of the implications of what Jesus has been trying to impress on his disciples.

By presenting a child as an icon of greatness, Jesus inverts the conventional estimates of honour in his society. Children had low social status, and the high infant mortality rate and low life expectancy combined to consign them to the weakest and most vulnerable sections of the community. Here they stand for the kingdom's vision of greatness, and they even represent the Messiah (v. 5). Their lowliness is a picture of the radical re-valuing of honour and blessing expressed in the Beatitudes, and exemplified by Jesus himself (11:29–30).

Disciples who accept Jesus' estimate of honour are rightly called 'little ones'. The Greek word behind the references to 'sin' in verses 6–9 is the same as in 16:23, when Jesus calls Peter a 'hindrance'—a 'stumbling block'. Disciples can trip over Jesus' hard words about the messianic way of rejection and suffering. Pressure can come from the outside world to conform to its estimates of greatness, and the Christian community can all too easily collude with these alien values. Hence Jesus' call to single-minded devotion, in vivid and colourful language that is designed to shock his followers out of any complacency (cf. 5:29–30).

Verses 10–14 echo Jesus' opening words about greatness. Those who adopt the messianic way should not become objects of contempt, because the heavenly Father shares Jesus' estimate of them. Belief in angelic mediation was common in contemporary Judaism: the 'little ones' are represented in heaven itself. And to the heavenly Father, even one of them who wanders off the messianic way is as precious as a lost sheep.

How far does today's Church reflect society's estimates of greatness and honour? What would it mean to hear and act on these words of Jesus?

3 The messianic way of church discipline
Read Matthew 18:15–35

Jesus now moves on to the specific issue of church discipline. The discourse appears to be addressed to the later Christian community rather than the group of disciples with him in Galilee.

Verse 17 assumes the existence of 'the church' (the word is only found here and in 16:18 in any of the Gospels). Verse 20 suggests that Jesus is physically absent, though present as the Church's risen Lord (compare 28:20). It is interesting to note that this verse envisages the presence of Jesus among his followers in the same way that rabbinic texts speak of the 'glory of God' (the *shekinah*) being present among those who gather to study the Jewish Law.

The word translated by 'sin' in verse 15 is different from that in verses 6–9. It carries the idea of offending against the community, rather than conforming to the world's way of estimating honour. Verses 15–17 set out a disciplinary practice which has parallels in the Jewish scriptures (Leviticus 19:17; Deuteronomy 19:15) and the Dead Sea Scrolls. First the matter is dealt with privately, then before two or three witnesses, and if this does not bring about repentance, only then is the matter set before the church. The whole process is intended to keep the offender inside the community—only if it fails is the 'brother' regarded as an outsider ('a Gentile and a tax collector') and expelled.

Jesus' words to Peter in 16:19 are repeated in verse 18, and applied to a wider group. The Church's decisions in these disciplinary cases will be ratified by heaven, insofar as it gathers 'in my name'—that is, under the authority of Jesus. The fact that Jesus' words about binding and loosing are spoken to those who are called to the messianic way says something about the exercise of disciplinary power in the Church. As with true greatness, so with discipline: the messianic way of Jesus challenges, and even inverts, worldly estimates and practices.

How can the Church sustain the responsibility Jesus gives it to do heaven's work on earth? How can it ensure that its disciplinary procedures are in keeping with 'blessed are the merciful'? Indeed, how far does mercy stretch? This is the substance of the question Peter asks on behalf of the Church. The parable in verses 23–35 uses fantastic numbers to make the point that mercy must flow from the heart. The first servant owed the equivalent of £2 billion, the second a mere £3,000! Yet the first servant mocked his master's generosity, and paid the price. The parable shows that in its difficult work of maintaining discipline, the Christian community must live as it prays: 'forgive us our sins, as we forgive those who sin against us'.

God's mercy must under no circumstances be mocked. There is nothing here to undermine the seriousness of the offence, but much to underline the high status of the offender.

4 The messianic people—gender and age
Read Matthew 19:1–15

Jesus now leaves Galilee and journeys south, to the region north of the Dead Sea. Though Matthew has nothing to compare with Luke's 'travel narrative' (9:51—19:44), Jesus is now clearly on the way to Jerusalem, and his final conflict with the Jewish leaders.

The Pharisees want to know Jesus' opinion on the disputed matter of divorce. They and he know that Moses allowed divorce (Deuteronomy 24:1–4), but Jewish scribes disagreed over the grounds. Some allowed divorce for trivial matters, others only in particular circumstances. Where does Jesus stand on this spectrum of interpretation? By referring the questioners to the creation stories in the scriptures, Jesus appeals to the Creator's intention 'from the beginning' (vv. 4, 6). But by bringing together Genesis 1:27 and 2:24, he strikes a body blow to the patriarchal system within which contemporary divorce law operated. If 'male and female' are made in God's image (some rabbis believed that only the man was made in God's image, and the woman in the image of the man!), and if husband and wife become 'one flesh', a woman should not be regarded as a man's property. A wife ought not to be disposed of like a field or traded like cattle. Jesus' teaching here is of a piece with his attitude towards other disadvantaged groups in his society. He sees the kingdom of heaven restoring the ideal order of creation within Israel—and in the messianic people of God, women and men belong equally.

According to verse 9, the only ground for divorce is 'unchastity', sexual unfaithfulness before or during the marriage (something that Joseph believed Mary was guilty of—see 1:18ff.). The disciples wonder whether Jesus is setting his sights too high. Are his high ideals so unattainable that it is better not to marry? The sayings about eunuchs in verses 11–13 are only found in this Gospel. The first two categories refer to accidents of birth and castration; the third uses the term as a metaphor for celibacy. High ideals for the relations between the sexes do not necessarily entail setting sexuality aside, as if there is no possibility of celebrating it as a gift of God. For the messianic people of God, celibacy can only ever be a vocation for the few.

Talk of the relations between the sexes leads naturally to the place of children. We have already seen the low estate of the child used as an icon of greatness and the epitome of humility. By welcoming the children in all their vulnerability and weakness, Jesus enacts his own teaching in the Beatitudes. If women and men belong equally in the messianic people of God, then so do children and adults.

5 The messianic people—wealth and prosperity
   Read Matthew 19:16—20:16

The reordering of values and priorities among God's messianic people continues in this section on wealth and prosperity. A rich man could properly expect to enjoy the blessings of the age to come ('eternal life' is best understood as 'life in the [new] age'), so the rich young man simply asks Jesus to confirm his hope. Jesus tells him that obedience rather than ownership guarantees future blessing. The list of commandments is slightly different in each of the Synoptic Gospels, though all agree that Jesus does not mention either the first four (which deal with the worship of God) or the tenth: 'you shall not covet'. Is this deliberate?

We should not underestimate what Jesus asks of the rich young man: to sell his family home and land, to break his kinship ties, to abandon all earthly security and join the little band whose leader had nowhere to lay his head (8:20) is a tall order. He is called to become a living icon of child-like discipleship (18:3; 19:14), with a perfection to match the generous mercy of the heavenly Father (5:48). His sorrowful departure reveals him as a man who foolishly thinks he can serve God and mammon (6:24), one whose 'delight in riches chokes the word' (13:22). If covetousness is idolatry (Colossians 3:5), then the man has made an idol of his prosperity. He worships his wealth rather than Israel's God.

Jesus' reflections on his meeting with the rich young man alarm the disciples. Who can be saved if not the rich? According to conventional estimates they above all people enjoy God's favour now. Will they not do so all the more in the age to come? Once again Jesus makes the point that earthly values must be judged by the kingdom of heaven. Verse 28 reflects the popular Jewish belief that Israel, or a righteous group within Israel, will share in God's judgment of the nations (see Daniel 7:13–14, 27). It is Jesus' disciples, who have given up so much to follow him, who can expect to share in the future's blessings—not the rich.

The 'reversal of values' theme persists into the parable of the labourers in the vineyard. The story reflects social and economic conditions in Palestine, where landless peasants waited for landowners to give them work as day labourers. Notice how those hired at the eleventh hour (5 p.m.) are not only paid the *same* as those who had worked all day, they are also paid *first*. The parable may not promote good labour relations or just working practices, but it forces home the point about the kingdom of heaven's inversion of earthly values.

6 The redeeming power of service *Read Matthew 20:17–34*

Jesus now has Jerusalem clearly in his sights as he tells his disciples for the third time about his impending passion. Even if the precise wording of verses 18–19 owes more to later reflection on the actual course of events, there are good reasons for believing that these words bring us close to the mind of Jesus as he anticipated what lay ahead of him.

Jesus could well be drawing on the imagery of the vision in Daniel 7 here. According to the Jewish historian Josephus, Jesus' contemporaries held that Daniel was a prophet for their time, although his book was written about 200 years earlier. In the vision, four menacing beasts symbolizing earthly rulers are stripped of their power, while 'one like a son of man', a human figure who represents 'the saints of the Most High' (Jews who remained faithful during a time of severe oppression), is vindicated by God. Jesus uses Daniel's vision to articulate his own faith. Despite the opposition he is about to face from the Jewish leaders in Jerusalem and the imperial forces who will collude with them by carrying out his crucifixion, he believes that God will stand by him and his cause. Notwithstanding the violence coming to him, he trusts that *his* vision of God's reign and *not theirs* will usher in the messianic kingdom—a conviction he will eventually press home before the high priest (26:64).

It is ironic that the mother's request for her sons (in Mark and Luke, James and John speak for themselves) follows on immediately from Jesus' most explicit statement about his passion. The disciples still cannot see that he simply does not fit the traditional messianic stereotype of a warrior king. The bravado in the two brothers' 'we are able' will soon be exposed as a reckless overestimate of the capabilities of their whole group. Jesus persists in trying to burst the bubble of their messianic fantasies, insisting that this Son of man is the very antithesis of those Gentile political leaders who like to throw their weight around. He has already used the child as an image of true greatness; here he adds the slave to the portrait gallery, to press home his point that messianic people must be willing to use their power for the benefit of others, not at their expense. Who better to exemplify this way of liberation from the destructive cycles of violence than the Son of man? He will continue to give up his life for others until he has no more to give.

As if to demonstrate his redeeming power, Jesus then heals two blind men who shout for help from the roadside. Their sight restored, they follow him on the way to Jerusalem. Coming so soon after the persistent spiritual blindness of the disciples, the opening of their eyes is a sign of hope that those who have journeyed with Jesus all the way from Galilee might come to 'see' the redeeming significance of his generous self-giving. Only as his disciples follow him into Jerusalem are the eyes of their faith eventually opened.

GUIDELINES

The Messiah triumphs by absorbing rejection and violence, not by retaliation. Greatness and blessing are estimated according to vulnerability and lowliness. Community leaders make mercy the measure of discipline. Gender, age and wealth have no power to shape the life of the people of God. According to the teaching of Jesus, these are the contours of the kingdom of heaven. Do they also indicate the shape of the landscape in today's Church?

Further reading

Margaret Davies, *Matthew*, JSNT, Sheffield Academic Press, 1993

Jack Dean Kingsbury, *Matthew as Story*, second edition, Fortress Press, 1988

Bruce J. Malina and Richard L. Rohrbaugh, *Social Science Commentary on the Synoptic Gospels*, Fortress Press, 1992

Graham Stanton, *A Gospel for a New People: Studies in Matthew*, T. & T. Clark, 1992

Esther

At first sight Esther seems an unlikely book to find in the Bible on several counts. It is an overtly secular book. It makes no mention of God, of prayer or of any religious observance, with the exception of fasting, the explanation perhaps for its absence from among the Dead Sea Scrolls. It seems, superficially at least, a nationalistic tale, ending on a note of vengeance. Our study of the book may lead us, however, not only to modify some of these first impressions but to be challenged by its message. For this is not simply a gripping story of intrigue and manoeuvre, of drama and suspense. It is a theological affirmation of the activity of God in history, hidden though it be, and of the supremacy of his wisdom and power beyond all human design or contrivance.

The book of Esther must be read not in isolation, but in the light of Jewish tradition. Like the Joseph and Exodus narratives it is a story of reversal, and who but God could work such dramatic deliverance for those at the very brink of extermination?

It is a story, too, of human courage and endeavour. Although by society's conventions at the time women were subject to men, the threatened annihilation of the Jewish people is averted by the co-operation of a man and a woman, Mordecai and Esther, working together as equals in mutual respect.

Like the book of Daniel, which follows it in the Hebrew Bible, it concerns Jews of the Diaspora, living within a pagan society; but whereas Daniel and his three friends adhere closely to Jewish dietary laws and maintain their customary religious practices despite threat to their lives, there appears nothing of this conflict of loyalties for Esther at the court of Ahasuerus, that is to say in the Hebrew text. For the ancient Greek version, known as the Septuagint, has a different, overtly religious tone, with numerous references to God and to prayer, and to Esther's unease in the Persian court. This text, with its six major additions and numerous variants elsewhere in the narrative, is accessible in English in the Apocrypha.

How much of the story is history? Despite some uncertainties it is widely agreed that it has a historical basis. Ahasuerus is to be identified with Xerxes who ruled Persia from 485–465BC. The background is authentic. The author is well acquainted with life at the Persian court and there are numerous Persian names.

The notes are based mainly on the Revised Standard Version although other translations are cited occasionally.

11–17 NOVEMBER

1 On winning and losing *Read Esther 1*

The narrative is about power, human power and its limits, even kingly power, and divine limitless power. Appropriately the story begins with a portrayal of royal magnificence befitting the ruler of the vast Persian empire. There are two banquet scenes (a recurring motif in the story and the setting for many a pivotal event), one for the élite, the other for the entire populace, rich and poor. For the men, that is; the women take second place. Queen Vashti's banquet is mentioned briefly, although significantly for the reader. It is held in 'the palace which belonged to King Ahasuerus' (v. 9). There is no forgetting who is lord and master.

At the first banquet Ahasuerus displays 'the splendour and pomp of his majesty'. At the second he wishes to display his beautiful queen. But even royal power has limits. Vashti has a mind of her own (did Ahasuerus anticipate trouble when he sent *seven* eunuchs?). No reason is given for her refusal. The early Aramaic paraphrase (the Targum) suggests it offended her modesty for she was to appear naked. But the Hebrew text has no such implication and is the more forceful for that. For the issue is not primarily one of modesty, but of Vashti's right as a woman not to be treated as an object, the king's possession. The king is non-plussed. The response of his advisors has ironical overtones. The honour of all husbands throughout the empire is at stake (v. 17). Vashti must be dismissed. The king goes to extreme lengths to safeguard male domination. Yet the heroine of the story is a woman of obscure background who, by an act of disobedience to the king (4:16), eventually saves her nation.

By her refusal to comply with the king's demand Vashti wins. Her will prevails against the king's, but her story and her victory remain her own, a private matter. It is Esther, criticized by some as a negative stereotype of womanhood, who ultimately overrides the conventions of society and, by her courage, dominates the story.

Within this first chapter sixteen names occur, mostly of minor characters. All the more surprising, then, that one name is missing throughout the book—God's name.

2 Esther the realist *Read Esther 2:1–18*

This is a chapter of contrasts: the powerful but indecisive king, his thoughts lingering on the past, dependent on the advice of others (v. 4); and Esther (her Hebrew name Hadassah means 'myrtle'), an orphaned exile who wins the king's love (v. 17) and, as the story unfolds, by courage and determination bends him to her will. The remark of an earlier commentator that Mordecai had the brains, Esther the beauty, is a caricature of the story.

Vashti must be replaced by another beautiful girl. Verse 4 is ambiguous, perhaps deliberately so, its meaning to be filled out as the story progresses. The girl to be chosen is to 'be queen', but the verb can also mean 'to reign', and Esther turns out to be queen in more than name. She truly exercises royal power. A massive beauty contest is arranged for the king's pleasure. Esther, criticized by some for 'playing the man's game', is no social climber. She has no choice but to conform to custom and obey the king's will. She obeys Mordecai, too, in concealing her Jewish birth (v. 10). Like Daniel and his friends, she quickly finds favour with those in charge. Verse 11 is significant: Mordecai is continually in proximity to the royal palace, and thereby hangs the tale.

Esther replaces Vashti. But immediately we sense a difference. Vashti's banquet in chapter 1 was a secondary matter; now the banquet for all the king's servants is emphatically 'Esther's banquet' (v. 18). She had won not only the king's favour but his devotion; he loved her (v. 17).

Esther is a realist. Acting within the structures of patriarchal society, valued for the beauty of her face and figure (v. 7), she transcends convention. The king, seeking physical beauty and sexual attraction, ironically meets in Esther the qualities of true womanhood. Esther wins, not for herself but for her people, and in the end the story is hers.

3 A plot discovered *Read Esther 2:19–23*

Up to this point we have met three of the main characters of the story: a monarch ruling over vast provinces stretching all the way from India to Ethiopia (more accurately northern Sudan, see GNB, rather than modern Ethiopia), a Jewish orphan girl totally subject to the king's will—not an attractive picture to the modern reader—and her uncle Mordecai whose care had brought her safely to womanhood. Like Esther, Mordecai has found favour at the Persian court. His place at the king's gate (v. 19) is not that of a beggar but of a court official, 'appointed by the king to an administrative position' (GNB). Esther's continued obedience to Mordecai is emphasized (v. 20). The interplay between obedience and disobedience is increasingly a prominent theme in the narrative. But Esther is more than her uncle's docile niece. She is his go-between to the king. When Mordecai discovers a plot by two palace eunuchs to assassinate Ahasuerus he tells it to *Queen* Esther. Her royal status is of crucial importance here. In warning the king of the danger Esther moves from a passive to an active role and becomes instrumental, with Mordecai, in saving the king's life.

The brief account of the treachery of Bigthan and Teresh seems, at first sight, a digression from the main story. It stands, however, at the heart of the drama. The foiling of the plot by Mordecai is the key which resolves the crisis to come. Two phrases are particularly significant: Esther told the king 'in the name of Mordecai', and the matter was 'recorded in the book of the annals in the presence of the king'. The execution which followed was no summary judgment. The matter was investigated carefully and found to be true (v. 23).

In chapter 2 the narrator skilfully prepares the reader for the events which follow. As there were two banquets in chapter 1 before 'Esther's banquet' (2:18), there are to be two further banquets in chapters 5 and 7 and two more scenes centred on the gallows (7:10; 9:13). Our author is an accomplished storyteller.

And now only the last of the four main characters in the drama remains to be introduced in the next chapter—Haman, the villain of the piece.

4 Riding for a fall *Read Esther 3*

This chapter is an all-male story with three sharply contrasting characters: the ruthless Haman promoted to chief minister, obsessed by pride of position, the obstinate Jew, Mordecai, the sole flaw in Haman's triumph: and, torn between them, the weak and easily manipulated king. This story is not about anti-Semitism. Not until Haman's personal pride is affronted by Mordecai's refusal to pay homage does hostility against the Jewish people surface. Sadly, not only ancient times have seen conflict, fuelled by powerful personal animosities, blazing into national or racial catastrophe to the anguish of the helpless, and often innocent, masses.

On a larger canvas, as the whole tale unfolds, Haman provides a foil to Esther. Their destinies are interwoven as his overweening pride plunges him from power into powerlessness and ultimately death, while Esther, risking all for her people's sake (4:16), rises from obscurity to royal authority (9:3). The irony is palpable. Chapter 1 purported to secure male predominance: wives were to be kept in subjection, each man by royal decree was to be master in his own house (1:22). The futility of that decree becomes apparent. Eventually Haman's wife, Zeresh, too, will figure in the story as a woman of authority (6:13).

Haman is wily and scheming but he is not unaware of the limits of human power. Mankind's destiny is seen as subject to fate, hence the careful casting of lots to determine the auspicious time for revenge on Mordecai and the annihilation of the Jews. Yet Haman has no inkling of that greater Power with whom we all must reckon, through whose mercy the day of doom will be turned into celebration and the victims become the victors.

Haman appeals to Ahasuerus' baser instincts. The profit motive (vv. 8–9) wins the day. The king abdicates responsibility. Entrusted with the royal signet, Haman has absolute power over the Jews (v. 11). Trenchant words heighten the drama as the chapter ends. The evil is contrived solely in high places, not with the connivance of the populace who emerge with greater honour than the nonchalant king and his chief minister: 'the king and Haman sat down to drink; but the city of Susa was perplexed' (v. 15).

5   Roles reversed! *Read Esther 4*

The chapter opens in a scene of paralysed, grief-stricken inactivity, the desolation of sackcloth and ashes, and Mordecai's 'wailing with a loud and bitter cry'. But the situation is transformed, and the chapter ends on a positive note through Esther's resolute courage. Both Vashti and Esther are heroines in their own right for each defied the powerful monarch in the interests of a higher morality. This is not simply a story of contrasts between two women, one disobedient, the other obedient. Vashti disobeyed, refusing to come to the king when summoned to his presence. Esther disobeyed, daring to come into the royal presence when uninvited. But the one was demoted for her disobedience, the other rewarded. Esther is wrongly devalued by those who regard her only as a negative stereotype, meekly accepting the demeaning conventions of a society which valued women primarily for their physical attributes. She is ready to put her life on the line, not like Vashti for her own honour but for the life of her people. In the end conventional Esther plays the more unconventional role. Mordecai obeys her orders (v. 17). Their roles are reversed. But none of this would have happened without their mutual trust and respect—or without the cooperation of others (vv. 4, 16).

And thus the narrator interweaves the themes of obedience and disobedience, and of the accountability of choice. Esther at the same time obeys and disobeys, choosing Mordecai's instructions against the king's sovereign will, though disobedience may mean death (v. 11). Here is commitment to a greater good. 'Who knows', says Mordecai, 'whether you have not come to the kingdom for such a time as this?' Behind Mordecai's question lies the hint of a deeper purpose. Some have taken the reference to 'another place' (v. 14) as a covert allusion to God.

Humanly speaking, Esther is in complete control, no longer passive as in chapter 1. She has made her choice: 'if I perish, I perish'. But she is not arrogantly self-sufficient. She requests a solemn fast as the pre-requisite for her action (v. 16).

The tension heightens. Esther takes her life in her hands and goes unbidden into the king's presence. The story in the Hebrew version is terse and unadorned. Some feminist commentators profess themselves dismayed that Esther should use her feminine charms when she confronts the king, but in fact there is little of this in the Hebrew text. To don her royal robes is not a matter of charm but of convention. The narrative is restrained; there is no emphasis on female wiles or on womanly weakness and fear.

The Greek version (included in the Apocrypha) contrasts strongly with this. Here Esther is undoubtedly a negative stereotype, a weak, helpless woman. She leans on her maid, faints at the sight of the king's anger. Her weakness and fear have the desired effect. A romantic scene follows. The king takes her into his arms and reassures her. Esther responds, 'I saw you, my lord, like an angel of God, and my heart was shaken with fear at your glory. For you are wonderful, my lord, and your countenance is full of grace.' The Esther of the Greek version is hardly a model of sincerity for it is in this version, unlike the Hebrew, that she speaks openly of her repugnance of life at the Persian court.

Not only does the Greek version represent Esther in ways more in accordance with conventional attitudes to women in patriarchal societies, it also introduces an overtly religious note, here and elsewhere, which is absent from the Hebrew text. Before she enters the king's presence, for example, she invokes 'the aid of the all-seeing God and Saviour'.

The story then takes a strange turn. Despite the king's generous offer to grant her petition even to the half of his kingdom, Esther makes a strange request (v. 4). The banquet motif of the earlier chapters reappears. Significantly, through this delay, unknown to Esther, Mordecai comes to the very brink of death (v. 14).

Throughout there is skilful depiction of human nature, the overweening pride which yet needs to bolster itself by boasting of its wealth and honours. Verse 9 carries an ominous hint of nemesis to come, and verse 14 of the overturning of human plans. There is irony too. The subjection of women was reinforced by royal decree (1:22), yet here is the king rewarding Esther for her disobedience, and Haman, too, taking orders from his wife (v. 14).

GUIDELINES

'Who knows whether you have not come to the kingdom for such a time as this?' (4:14).

Reflect on Mordecai's words to Esther as both challenge and encouragement in your own situation in the light of God's purpose.

> *Lord, we give ourselves to you*
> *for the cause of your glorious kingdom,*
> *for joy or for sorrow,*
> *for success or for failure,*
> *for life or for death,*
> *now and evermore.*

18–24 NOVEMBER   ESTHER 6–10

1   The danger of injured pride *Read Esther 6*

This is a chapter of high drama. It begins with the kind of gloating arrogance which only the totally self-centred can know. It ends in devastating humiliation. On the human level there is extraordinary coincidence. Ordinary events (the king's sleeplessness, the reading of the archives, Haman's arrival in the courtyard) come together with extraordinary results. The plot is foiled and its intended victim raised to honour. But the story demands to be understood on an altogether deeper level. Not random chance but divine purpose is behind it. Through two small but significant additions the Greek version makes explicit what is implicit in the Hebrew—God is at work. In verse 1, what appears as coincidence becomes, in the Greek text, divine action: '...the Lord kept the king from sleeping', and in verse 13 to the words 'you [Haman] will surely fall before him [Mordecai]', the Greek adds 'for the living God is with him'.

In this chapter we meet Zeresh again, the third woman in the Esther story. Like Esther and Vashti she is no passive figure but an active participant in the drama. Unlike them, however, she has no mind of her own. Her advice to Haman is coloured by her companions of the moment: in 5:14, in company with his friends, she encourages him in vengeance; in 6:13, in the company of wise men, she speaks not only wisely but prophetically and with unconscious irony. Haman, enraged because Mordecai would not fall in homage before him, is himself about to fall before his enemy.

The chapter is about power—the limitations of arrogant human power, and the prevailing power of God who is no less present in human affairs because of his hiddenness. Human responsibility, the need for cooperation between men and women, the challenge to courageous action have been the themes of earlier chapters, but these of themselves are insufficient to shape events. There is a dark side to the story as there is to human experience—the extent of the evil which can be planned, if not perpetrated, through the wicked scheming of one man. Hope lies only in God.

2 Disclosures! *Read Esther 7:1—8:2*

The dramatic tension is sustained. The king and Haman relax after their meal, savouring their wine (v. 2). But the king knows that serious business is afoot, for is this not Esther's *second* pressing invitation to a banquet? He addresses her not with familiarity but with her full royal title, Queen Esther, and solemnly promises the fulfilment of her request (as in 5:3). Esther answers with full attention to oriental court etiquette (contrast Haman's brusque answer in his arrogance in 6:7). With verse 4 comes the first intimation to the king and Haman of Esther's Jewish nationality, and with it the disclosure that the king himself, all unawares, has been involved in the plot which would have spelt death to his queen and to the very man, Mordecai, to whom he owed his own life. Esther's plea sounds simple and unadorned, but it is not without artifice. She understands the king and, just as Haman did in 3:9, appeals to the ever powerful profit motive, the financial loss to the king entailed in the destruction of her people. Here again we notice a touch of extreme exaggeration which can hardly represent realistically Esther's own emotions: 'our affliction is not to be compared with the loss to the king' (v. 4).

Then comes the startling disclosure to the king of the enemy's identity which the reader has known all along. The scene is simply portrayed but all the human emotions are there: terror, agitated anger, a desperate plea. The situation is ironical. The man who, a few moments before, had held the life or death of the Jews in his grasp now has to plead with a Jewish woman for his own survival (7:7).

Echoes of the Joseph story force themselves on our notice. There Potiphar's wife, with evil intent, misrepresents the situation and Joseph suffers the consequence for alleged seduction (Genesis 39:17–20). Here the king misinterprets Haman's desperate bid for his life as an attempt to violate the queen. Haman's fate is sealed. The gallows is already prepared—by his own hand (5:14). Here is a double irony. Haman's house (his whole estate) becomes Esther's, and his authority as chief minister to use the king's seal is conferred on Mordecai. But Esther's own authority is not minimized. She it is who puts Mordecai in charge of Haman's property (8:1–2).

3   Evil negated *Read Esther 8:3–8*

Here is the crucial test of Esther's character. She and Mordecai are safe. They have been honoured by the king. Their enemy's position and possessions have come into their hands and he is no more. But Esther does not seek self-glory. Her concern is for her people, for commitment to God, as the prophets said, is not a private matter. This is why Paton's disparaging view of Esther (*International Critical Commentary*, 1908) is unjustified, that 'Esther, for the chance of winning wealth and power, takes her place in the herd of maidens who became concubines of the king'.

This is where the importance of taking the story on its own terms becomes clear. Esther is a realist who works resolutely for justice within the situation in which she finds herself, or rather, as the implication of the entire story leads us to acknowledge, the place in which God has placed her. Her pleas to the king this time are accompanied by tears and obeisance at his feet (v. 3). Her tone too, 'how can I endure to see the calamity that is coming to my people?' (v. 6), differs strikingly from her words in 7:4, where it was politic to speak in terms of the king's loss. In the light of the king's earlier response there is less need now for dissembling. It is only at this point in the Hebrew story that we glimpse something of Esther's emotions, for the narrative is devoid of the sentimental.

The edict issued by Haman under the king's seal is irrevocable (v. 8). It can only be negated by a further edict of equal authority, this time from Esther and Mordecai who have authority to write in the king's name under his seal. Once again the king is seen in a pathetic light, disinclined to take action himself and deputing it to others.

The designation of Haman as 'the Agagite' (v. 3) is significant. It is reminiscent of the story in 1 Samuel 15 where Agag is the enemy of Israel (vv. 32–33). But it is not a matter of the sins of an ancestor being visited on him. Haman's destruction of the Jews would have outclassed that of his ancestor. From a purely private grudge against one man, Mordecai, his hatred has turned against a whole race living peaceably within society, a warning of what the human heart is capable. Yet the dark side of life is not the last word. God is above and beyond, 'and his mercy is over all his works' (Psalm 145:9).

4   The great reversal *Read Esther 8:9–17*

The name Sivan, the third month of the year (May–June), occurs only here in the Old Testament and was one of the Babylonian names which came into use in Israel after the exile in the sixth century BC. Just as the first edict (3:12) had been framed by Haman not by the king, so the second edict is drawn up by Mordecai. Powerful monarch though Ahasuerus was, he remains a passive figure in the story. The edict was written by professional scribes and promulgated as before in the many languages of the peoples under Persian rule, this time including Hebrew. There are interesting glimpses here of the care taken with the royal mail— swift horses bred for the purpose of speedy communication over vast distances.

The language used, 'destroy, slay, annihilate' (v. 11), is identical to that of Haman's decree (cf. 3:13). In that instance, however, the destruction was without provocation. Here permission is granted to the Jews for defence only, 'to gather and defend their lives' if attacked by an armed force. The reference to 'children and women' in verse 11 is ambiguous and open to misinterpretation (in contrast to 3:13, where young and old are specifically included in the slaughter). In some English translations (e.g. NEB, REB, GNB) it is taken to mean that the Jews are to be permitted to slay not only those guilty of attacking them, but the wives and children of the attackers too. On rational grounds, however, it is unlikely that Ahasuerus would have given such broad licence for slaughter of the people of his empire. It is equally justifiable on grammatical grounds, and from its position in the Hebrew sentence preferable, to take the phrase to refer to the wives and children of the Jews who are attacked (as does NIV) and whose goods are taken as booty.

Verse 15 indicates that there was no widespread anti-Semitic feeling in Susa. Just as its citizens had been perplexed at Haman's edict against the Jews (3:15), so now they rejoice with the Jewish population at Mordecai's elevation to be the king's chief minister. The Jewish community, far from being decimated by slaughter find their numbers increased by the addition of Gentile converts (v. 17).

5 Self-defence, not greed for gain *Read Esther 9:1–19*

There is reason to suggest, as a number of scholars have argued, that the original narrative ended with chapter 8 on a note of joy, without the bloodshed which we find so offensive in chapter 9. Certainly what follows lacks the dramatic quality of the previous chapters and has the feel of a pedestrian rounding off of events. The repetition of the death of Haman's sons (compare v. 10 with v. 14) also suggests layers of later additions to the narrative. Yet, whether this is so or not, we cannot escape the fact that the book as we have it in Jewish and Christian scripture includes chapter 9. What are we to make of it?

The whole story has been one of dramatic reversal: a queen dethroned, an orphan crowned, a villain unmasked, his victim honoured. The present chapter drives the point home: the very day appointed for destruction becomes for the Jews a day of triumph (v. 2). What follows is abhorrent to us, but it must be read with due attention to its context. This is neither indiscriminate slaughter nor vengeance, but the removal of those who threatened

Jewish existence (v. 5). It is not a matter of racial hatred, of Jew pitted against Gentile, for Persians, too, sided with the Jews (v. 3).

Inevitably we feel disappointment that, after all the nobility of her character, it is Esther who requests from the king further opportunity to hunt down their enemies (v. 13). Nor does verse 16 make pleasant reading, but it must be noted that 'they gathered to defend their lives' and gain 'relief from their enemies'. Such are the exigencies of life. The pages of history tell many a tale of ruthless cruelty, and who can say that events of our present decade are in any way superior? The repeated emphasis on the fact that the Jews took no plunder (vv. 10, 15–16) reiterates that it was not for gain but solely for life and future that they acted.

One can sense the relief in verse 22 of those whose lives had been lived under the shadow of hatred and fear when sorrow was turned into gladness, mourning into a holiday. There is no tone here of gloating over the slaughter of enemies, but celebration to mark deliverance.

As Christians we cannot but abhor violence, but it ill behoves those of us who have never lived under threat of annihilation to our whole community to condemn those who have suffered unimaginable terrors and who wish, by whatever means, to secure for their children a safer, happier life.

6 The Purim festival *Read Esther 9:20—10:3*

From verse 23 onwards we find a summary of what has gone before. The narrative skill of the storyteller has gone. In place of the drama of the previous chapters there is rather tedious repetition. It is here that we have the association of the story of Esther with the Jewish festival of Purim (celebrated annually February–March), linked here with the fact that Haman had cast a lot (*pur*) to determine the day of annihilation (v. 26).

To the end of chapter 9 Esther's authority is emphasized and at her command the celebration is inaugurated. The brief conclusion in chapter 10, however, reverts to the deeds of Ahasuerus chronicled in the royal archives of Media and Persia, a characteristic formula at the end of a king's reign found frequently throughout the books of Kings (see also 1 Chronicles 29:29). Attention turns from Esther to Mordecai. The courageous woman whose resourcefulness saved her nation is once more eclipsed by the figure of her uncle Mordecai. The equality and cooperation of men and women as equals has receded before the conventions of patriarchal society. Yet nevertheless the story is Esther's and to this the title of the book in our scriptures gives lasting testimony. The whole of chapter 10 is phrased in the masculine: 'brethren', 'his people', 'his descendants' (v. 3). Perhaps this underlines for us how remarkable it is that Esther's story has been told at all and preserved over more than two millennia.

GUIDELINES

The book of Esther is both an exciting and an uncomfortable story for the Christian reader. As part of holy scripture it cannot be ignored, but it must be read with discernment. It is not intrinsically a narrowly nationalistic book, for had such been its purpose it would surely, as a book which delights in names, have named the name of Israel's covenant God, Yahweh. The Jewish people of the Diaspora are depicted as existing peaceably with Gentiles under Persian rule. Not until one man's pride is injured does hatred show its face and conflict arise. Like much of the Old Testament, the book of Esther roots us in the real world where, still today, life is threatened and the possibility of genocide is a reality.

History is the story of human causality. Evil's effects ripple on long after its perpetrator has gone—and so do the effects of good. From this perspective God is often the hidden God, as Esther's story reminds us. But, to faith, the Lord of history is never the absent God, unmindful of human suffering. Without relieving humans of their responsibility, he wields ultimate control. Yet, in the light of twentieth-century history, with its still undimmed memories of the holocaust, this raises for us theological questions. How are realism and faith to co-exist?

Perhaps something of an answer comes from the following courageous affirmation of faith in an inscription found on a cellar wall in Cologne where Jews had been hiding from the Nazis:

I believe in the sun even when it is not shining.
I believe in love even when feeling it not.
I believe in God even when he is silent.

Further reading

J. Baldwin, *Esther*, Tyndale Press, 1984

J.G. McConville, *Ezra, Nehemiah and Esther*, Westminster Press, Philadelphia, 1985

A.M.Rodriguez, *Esther: A Theological Approach*, Andrews University Press, Michigan, 1995

Selected Psalms

Our use of the Psalms in worship or private prayer is often hurried. In worship, if we are required to say alternate verses of a psalm together with other members of the congregation, we may have to pay more attention to getting the words right than to thinking about their meaning. This habit of hurried recitation can then be easily taken over into private prayer! The opportunity to spend more time on the Psalms via *Guidelines* is thus a precious one, but it brings its own problems. While we are hurriedly skipping through verses in public worship we can overlook the many difficult sentiments that they contain and fasten upon their noble and sublime expressions of trust and praise. A deeper reflection upon the Psalms, however, confronts us with the fact that noble and problematic sentiments come together more often than is comfortable.

In making a selection of psalms for *Guidelines* in the pre-Christmas season, I have deliberately chosen some of the most difficult ones in the whole Psalter. Their difficulty lies in their often uncharitable and vindictive thoughts about the godless and the enemies of the psalmists. How we can handle these passages, and how they might be understood in the light of Christmas, will be the aim of the comments that are offered. The translation used is the Revised English Bible (REB).

---

25 NOVEMBER–1 DECEMBER

1 The power of words Read Psalm 12

We know nothing about how books were published or information was disseminated in ancient Israel. At the least the Hebrew language was written in an alphabet of twenty-two letters, as opposed to the 300–600 signs used for Babylonian and Assyrian, and this meant that literacy in Israel was not confined to a handful of specialists. We do not, however, know anything about reading habits in Israel. In spite of this, it is clear from our psalm that the power of words was as important in Israel as it is in our own word-saturated society.

The psalmist describes a situation where communication has broken down because the use of words has been corrupted. People lie to each other, and words spoken mask a deceitful underlying reality (v. 2). There appears to be a group that has power over words, to the disadvantage of others (v. 4). Perhaps by well-organized rumour, or perhaps by skilful propagation of half-truths that arouse the prejudices of hearers, this party manipulates and distorts the truth on behalf of its own interests. The losers are the poor, by which we should understand not only the economically poor, but the powerless against whom false accusations are made or those who are exploited by the rumours that are spread about.

The psalmist contrasts this false, human, use of words with the words that come from God (v. 6). Words spoken by prophets may be in mind here. God's words contain no deceit. Such is their integrity and reliability that they are like precious metals that have had all the dross removed by being heated in a crucible. Often, they may be harsh and uncomfortable words, especially if they condemn the people and the rulers on account of their deceit. They are also promises that give hope to the victims of false use of words (v. 5).

The manipulation of words in the interests of political or economic groups is a depressing feature of our modern world. This process dehumanizes us, and we long for leaders who will speak the truth. For our part, we should be committed to utter honesty, and should hope in God, whose incarnate word, Jesus Christ, is without spot or blemish.

2 Anguish in exile *Read Psalms 42 and 43*

Although Psalms 42 and 43 appear as two separate psalms in the traditional Hebrew text, some modern translations (e.g. REB) treat them as one psalm, while other translations (e.g. the Good News Bible) note that Psalm 43 continues Psalm 42. The New International Version states that, in many Hebrew manuscripts, the two psalms appear as one. This fact is important for interpretation. Read on its own, Psalm 42 gives us no clue about why the psalmist is in exile. Taken with Psalm 43, there is a hint that the psalmist may be the victim of false accusations (43:1).

The setting of the psalms appears to be near Mount Hermon, in what today is Lebanon, where the melting snows contribute to the springs that feed the river Jordan (42:6). The torrents crashing down the slopes of the mountains, which to us today might be a thrilling sight, filled the psalmist with foreboding, and reminded him forcefully of the troubles—both inner and outer—that assailed him.

What were these troubles? The outer ones are his banishment from the temple and its worship, which the psalmist remembers with longing and affection. Whether he was a priest or other temple official is not clear. It is interesting that the psalmist's wish to be back in the temple is not in order to offer sacrifice, but to take part in the festal worship of praise and thanksgiving.

The psalmist's inner turmoils lead to a sublime paradox at the heart of the psalm. Away from the temple, the psalmist feels banished from God's presence (42:2); yet the refrain (found at 42:5; 42:11 and 43:5) is an affirmation of hope in God in the midst of human anguish.

The psalm abounds in poetic allusions. The crashing torrents contrast with the quietly running streams sought by the hind, and with the tears that become the psalmist's food in his distress. The great Hermon mountain range inspires the image of God as a reliable rock (42:9).

The psalmist's prayer culminates in the request for God's light and truth to guide him back to God's holy hill. This will involve the refutation of the false accusations and of the lies told against him (43:1) which may have caused his banishment. Our world is not unfamiliar with people imprisoned on behalf of the truth, or of a misuse of words and power that result in the innocent being distanced from their access to God.

3   Betrayal by a friend *Read Psalm 55*

'Oh for the wings of a dove!' These words, immortalized in a famous recording, give no hint of the actual situation of anguish in which they are expressed. We all feel that we need to get away from things occasionally as we try to cope with the pressures of life, but the situation of the psalmist is not just the need for such a break. The psalmist speaks of being panic-stricken, torn with anguish, weighed down with the terrors of death, assailed by fear and trembling. As so often in the Psalms, although the complaints are specific, they are not sufficiently detailed for us to link them with a particular individual. Thus, attempts to relate this Psalm to incidents in the life of David or of Jeremiah are not entirely successful. The Psalm is sufficiently vague for it to be applicable to anyone who is in great danger and distress.

In verse 9 we have the first of several passages (see also vv. 15, 23) in which the psalmist hopes or declares that God will punish his enemies. Verses such as these offend modern readers as not being in harmony with New Testament teaching about forgiving one's enemies. But we need to ask ourselves the following questions: Does my life consistently conform to the standards set by the teaching of Jesus? If I were in the same situation as the psalmist, would I react any differently?

Part of the anguish of the psalmist stems from the fact that one of his enemies had once been a close friend (vv. 12–14). Friendships that turn to enmity are particularly hard to cope with, because in friendships we admit people to parts of our lives that are otherwise private property. The sense of betrayal is aggravated by this.

However, the psalm moves from its opening anguish and its later feeling of betrayal to an affirmation of hope and trust in God. However fickle human friends may be, God remains faithful to us, even when we betray him. Thus, in the midst of people whose words mask their true and evil intentions (vv. 19b–21), the psalmist affirms that God will sustain him and not let him be shaken (v. 22). There is no need, after all, to escape on the wings of a dove.

4 Wickedness in high places *Read Psalm 58*

In 1913 a commission was set up by the Archbishop of Canterbury to report on the translation and use of the Psalms in public worship. Among its recommendations in 1916 was the suggestion that certain psalms or verses should be omitted as unsuitable in public worship. The Psalter in the Prayer Book, as proposed in 1928, put this suggestion into effect by placing square brackets around some passages, indicating that they could be omitted at the discretion of the minister. The whole of Psalm 58 was placed in square brackets—a procedure also followed in the *Alternative Service Book* of 1980.

It is easy to see why Psalm 58 was treated like this. Not only does it contain some difficult and obscure Hebrew; it expresses some of the most vindictive sentiments found anywhere in the Bible, as well as images such as the 'deaf asp which stops its ears' (v. 4) which seems almost comic to modern readers. However, to lose this Psalm would be most unfortunate.

The Psalm begins with a difficulty in the Hebrew. Older translations address the opening question to 'the congregation', but modern versions such as the Revised English Bible and the New International Version take the Hebrew word to mean mighty or powerful people, and thus judges or (better) rulers. This gives an insight into the psalm and its vindictive sentiments. Absolute power corrupts absolutely, and the modern world has seen, and still sees, instances of this. What do you do when you live in a totalitarian society where there is no freedom of speech and only official lies and injustice? The psalmist's language does not exaggerate when it speaks of abusers of absolute power as wicked from birth (v. 3), and incapable of ever hearing any point of view but their own (cf. vv. 4–5).

In such a situation where there is apparently no prospect of human forces breaking the power of the rulers, the psalmist calls upon God to intervene, and in so doing he employs a series of remarkable images in verses 6–9. The wicked rulers are likened to lions whose teeth will be broken, to archers whose arrows kill their own soldiers, to aborted and stillborn children, and weeds and thorns that are uprooted. The image of the righteous bathing their feet in the blood of the wicked may offend us, but it expresses poetically the mixed feelings of relief and anger that people have felt when dictators have been deposed and freedom has been experienced.

5   Why do the wicked prosper? *Read Psalm 73*

The psalms that we have read up to now have seen the psalmist surrounded by enemies who, in some cases, have exiled the psalmist or have threatened his life. In today's psalm the psalmist faces the problem of indifference. If anything is under threat it is not so much his physical existence as his faith in a God of justice. Two factors put this faith under pressure. The first is the prosperity of the wicked, who appear to be not only wealthy and well nourished, but who seem to be spared the problems of daily life that affect ordinary people. The second factor is the manifest contempt of the wicked for any idea that justice matters, or that God's justice will ultimately prevail.

The psalmist's anguish is increased by the fact that the success of the wicked leads to their popularity, while the psalmist is possibly chided for trying to do what is right (v. 14) and is certainly inwardly tortured by the possibility that his loyalty to God has been pointless (v. 13).

On the face of it, and judged by common sense, the wicked are right and the psalmist is wrong. This is changed, however, when the psalmist goes to the sanctuary and in prayer and worship encounters God in such a way that his faith is renewed (v. 17). He realizes first of all that by leaving God out of his reasoning about the prosperity of the wicked, he was not doing justice to himself as a human being (vv. 21–22). For, to be truly human, a person needs to be in communion with God; and God is not only the God of the present world, but of the age to come. In verse 24 we have a rare glimpse in the Old Testament of a hope beyond death, in the idea that fellowship with God established in this world cannot be broken by death. This leads the psalmist to affirm that all his hope is founded on God alone (v. 25) and that this certainty will endure when all else has passed away (v. 26).

But if what endures is our hope in God, then it follows that those who have scorned God and mocked at his justice have nothing to hope for. Reality is very different from how it appears to the scoffers and their supporters. The psalmist does not gloat about the apparent fate of the ungodly (cf. vv. 18–20, 27) but reflects upon it rather soberly. From God's point of view, even the scoffers are his children, which is why Christ came into the world to seek and save the lost.

6 Twilight of the gods *Read Psalm 82*

Ancient Israelites were aware that other nations worshipped gods different from the God of Israel. Often in the Old Testament the Israelites themselves turned to foreign gods. Also, it is acknowledged in the Old Testament that other gods can be powerful (cf. 2 Kings 3:26–27 where the king of Moab offers his son as a sacrifice to Kemosh). Another strand in the Old Testament sees the gods of other nations as heavenly beings each of whom is responsible for overseeing the affairs of a nation (Deuteronomy 32:8–9).

In Psalm 82 God calls the gods of the nations to account. The charge against them is that they have not ensured that the fatherless, the destitute, the weak and the needy have been protected from the wicked. Neither have these vulnerable people been treated justly (vv. 3–4). The reason for this inaction is said to be ignorance (v. 5), which is hardly a divine virtue, and is thus part of the reason why these gods are sentenced to death. The psalmist sees no hope for a world whose foundations are giving way (v. 5), except in the rule of the God of Israel (v. 8).

At first sight this Psalm has little to do with our world, yet if we describe as 'gods' the forces that dominate and shape today's world we shall not stray too far from what the Psalm is about. The ruthless quest for material wealth that damages the environment, treats human employees as disposable items, and which depends upon the poverty of the Two-Thirds World; the process which puts the control of television and newspapers into the hands of a few individuals; the currency speculators who can take on a nation and force it to change its economic policies—these are just some examples of present-day 'gods' that shape the destinies of the nations and have no concern for the modern equivalents of the fatherless, the afflicted and the destitute. The values of God are utterly different; and in Jesus, God lived not among the powerful but the powerless in order to redeem the world.

GUIDELINES

Our readings have had much to say about the abuse of power, not only by rulers, but also by a former close friend who betrayed a trust. The currency of words is devalued, and even logic seems to be on the side of the ungodly who affirm that God is either blind to injustice or powerless to stop it. The 'answer' to these problems lies in prayer and worship; in experiencing the faithfulness of God in such a way that we know that God's promises can be relied upon, and that his kingdom has both come in Jesus Christ and will one day embrace all other forms of rule and authority.

2–8 DECEMBER

---

1 Without hope? *Read Psalm 88*

This psalm has been described as the saddest psalm in the whole Psalter. It appears to contain no glimmer of hope, and is almost a catalogue of woes and complaints. The psalmist is, or feels himself to be, on the brink of death (v. 3), which is not only a gloomy prospect in itself but is made more desperate by the thought that the shadowy existence vouchsafed to the dead in Sheol is one in which God cannot be known (vv. 10–12).

Another factor which adds to the darkness of this psalm is that the psalmist seems to have been in trouble ever since he was born (v. 15). Now, seemingly close to death, not only does he find it hard to draw near to God (v. 14), but is isolated from human companionship, believing that God has taken away from him his friends and neighbours (v. 18).

As with so many psalms, the details are not specific enough for us to identify the psalmist or his circumstances. On many occasions, I have read this psalm to students while in the cistern prison that is in the depths of St Peter in Gallicantu in Jerusalem, and I have asked them to imagine what it must have felt like to be in the utter darkness and filth of such a place, as Jeremiah was, for example (Jeremiah 38:6). That the psalm relates to such an experience is, however, only a guess.

For our purposes, the remarkable thing is that the psalm has been included in the Bible at all. It says much for the honesty and realism of the compilers that they have allowed this prayer of seeming utter hopelessness to survive. In doing so, they have given hope to later users of the psalm. First, if any reader feels anything like the psalmist does—that life is a sea of troubles and faith does not particularly help in coping with them—at least that reader is not the first or only person to have had that experience. Secondly, the psalmist's feelings are not the only clue to reality. The pessimism of Psalm 88 is followed by the confident opening of Psalm 89. Whatever individuals may feel at particular times, there *is* hope, as the accumulated experience of the community of faith as expressed in the Psalms shows clearly.

2 Reproof to injustice *Read Psalm 94*

This psalm resembles some others that we have read in that the psalmist is confronted by rulers who practise injustice. The widow, the stranger and the fatherless are being put to death (v. 6), and although those responsible deny that God either knows or cares about their misdeeds (v. 7), they are concerned to conceal their evil under the cloak of legality. They continue mischief under cover of law (v. 20).

The response of the psalmist is more active than in any of the psalms read so far. First, he deploys an intellectual argument. If the rulers believe in God at all, they can hardly maintain that he is indifferent to injustice. He gave to the human race the ability to hear and see: is God then deaf and blind? He is the author of human knowledge: is he then ignorant (vv. 9–10)? Secondly, the psalmist is convinced that justice is not merely something wanted by him personally, but that it is the concern of all the 'upright in heart' (v. 15). Thirdly, the psalmist takes strength from his fellowship with God and the inner conviction that this brings that the evil rulers are wrong about God, and that justice will prevail.

Whatever the original situation may have been which produced this psalm (again, the details are too vague to make a convincing answer possible), it is a composition that has much to say to today's world. The twentieth century has seen, and still sees, régimes in which people have been wrongly killed and imprisoned in the name of legality. The century has also witnessed the collapse of many of these régimes as the 'upright in heart' have insisted that 'justice should be joined to right' (v. 15). The eye of faith perceives behind such outcomes not simply the triumph of the human spirit, but the work of God who is the source of all the most noble aspirations of the human race.

3 Rebounding judgment *Read Psalm 109*

This is another psalm that fared badly at the hands of those who proposed the Prayer Book in 1928. Verses 5–19 in the Prayer Book version (vv. 6–20 in REB) were placed in brackets, a procedure also adopted by the *Alternative Service Book* of 1980 and the popular Franciscan publication, *Celebrating Common Prayer* (1992).

It has to be admitted that the verses thus designated contain a pretty comprehensive list of misfortunes that the psalmist wishes to see fall upon his enemies. These range from their premature death leaving the children fatherless (v. 9) to the financial ruin of the survivors and the obliteration of any memory of them (vv. 11, 13–15). To some extent, verses 8–15 can be understood in terms of the laws of evidence in ancient Israel. For a person to be convicted of an offence in a court, two witnesses were needed whose evidence agreed. But what if their evidence was false? We know from the story of Naboth (1 Kings 21) that a man could be executed and lose his property on the evidence of false witnesses. The Old Testament therefore laid down stringent rules about the penalties for giving false evidence (cf. Deuteronomy 19:16–21). If found guilty, a false witness suffered the same penalty that would have befallen the wrongly accused innocent man, had the latter been found guilty. Verses 8–15, then, may represent the kind of penalties that would have been applied to the innocent psalmist if his false accusers had succeeded in getting him convicted.

But there is more to the psalm than this. The enemy (or enemies) of the psalmist is portrayed as disloyal, persecuting and cursing, and the psalmist desires that these actions done to others will become part of his very being (v. 18); that he will be a curse to himself.

How do we deal with sentiments such as these? First, we should not condemn them in such a way as to suppose that we would feel and speak differently if we were in the psalmist's situation. How do we know that we would not feel the same resentment against false accusers? Secondly, we can bring these words before God as members of a deeply flawed human race, sharing to some extent in the deceitfulness and resentment which find such naked expression in the psalm. For it is only when we come before God, hiding nothing, that we can say with the psalmist, 'deal with me as befits your honour' (v. 21).

4   Certain of victory? *Read Psalm 129*

In this psalm the psalmist, speaking in the name of the whole people past and present, affirms that any defeats of the nation at the hands of an enemy have been only temporary. God has always ultimately vindicated his people (vv. 1–2). The story of Israel and Judah as related in the Bible richly illustrates this theme. Among victors over Israel were the Philistines in the time of Saul, the Syrians in the time of Elisha, and the Assyrians during the reign of Ahaz and Hezekiah. If this psalm was composed after the Babylonian exile, the further dimension is added that a defeat that should have been terminal for the existence of the nation, involving as it did the destruction of Jerusalem and the temple, was only an interlude in the ongoing story of the people. The psalmist compresses together some vivid images in verses 3–4: injuries inflicted upon a defeated soldier are likened to a farmer driving deep furrows into the the earth. God is likened to someone cutting free a prisoner bound by ropes or chains.

In verses 5–8 we meet a problem of translation that affects the interpretation. English translations take these verses to be a prayer about disasters that the psalmist wishes to fall on the enemies of Zion. However, some commentators and some translations into other European languages take the verse to be a statement which affirms that those who hate Zion will never ultimately prevail. Again, the psalmist's language is economical in the way in which poetic images are employed. From the image of grass growing on a roof that will quickly wither in the heat of the sun, the thought moves to the greeting exchanged between people at the time of the grain harvest.

If the psalm presents a problem to modern readers it should not be so much because of the sentiments of verses 5–8. Rather, the difficulty should lie in the implication of the psalm that God ultimately gives victory to Israel because Israel is Israel. However, the Old Testament taken as a whole never sees the vindication of Israel simply as the vindication of a people regardless of its attitude to justice and mercy. On the contrary, Israel's defeats were seen as God's acts of reproof against the injustices fostered by the nation. Only when we rise above sectional and national interests can we understand the way of a God who has no favourites, because he is concerned for the whole of humankind.

5 True victory *Read Psalm 130*

In many ways this psalm is the ideal complement to Psalm 129. The unbounded optimism of that psalm is replaced here by a deep sense of humility that enables the psalmist to discover the only ground for hope, namely, the mercy of God.

As so often, we cannot identify the situation that led to the psalm's composition, but this makes it suitable for use in many circumstances. The 'depths' of verse 1 are watery depths, which so often in the Old Testament stand for chaos and danger. Whatever those depths may be, they do not cut the psalmist off from prayer to God; but they do have the effect of making the psalmist aware of weakness and unworthiness. This produces a noble utterance (v. 3), which begins by being counter-factual. The psalmist reflects on how bad things would be if God were to keep an account of sins; no one would have any hope. Yet this is precisely what God does (cf. Psalm 94:9–11) *and*, at the same time, he is a God who forgives (v. 4). This realization brings the psalmist to awe and reverence before God.

Still, presumably, in the midst of the depths from which he cries, the psalmist waits in expectation for God's deliverance. He is like a watchman on night watch who longs eagerly to see the first light of dawn. (There is no morning twilight in Israel. The sun appears over the horizon with hardly any warning).

In the last two verses it may be that the psalmist has now been delivered and that he thus encourages the people to trust in God. The words in verse 8 'He alone' are emphatic. The whole psalm remains an object lesson in discovering our human weakness so that we come to rely solely on God's strength.

6 A cry for vengeance *Read Psalm 137*

This psalm falls into two distinct parts: verses 1–6 which recount how the exiles from Jerusalem felt when they were taken to Babylon in or after 587; and verses 7–9 which call for revenge upon Edom and Babylon. The Prayer Book, as proposed in 1928, and other service books place verses 7–9 in brackets.

The opening verses were not necessarily composed in Babylon. The word 'there' in verse 2 and the past tenses suggest that the psalmist has returned from exile and is recounting the anguish that is felt by the community as they contemplate a Jerusalem that lies in ruins. Verses 5–6 then have the sense: 'If I *ever* forget you, Jerusalem, may my right hand wither.'

Verses 7–9 are offensive to modern readers, especially the injunction to dash the babies of Babylon against a rock. Christian interpretation has tried to cope with these sentiments by spiritualizing them. Thus the rock has been interpreted as meaning Christ (cf. 1 Corinthians 10:4) and the babies have been understood as sins or unworthy thoughts. However much this approach may have satisfied people in the past (see C.S. Lewis, *Reflections on the Psalms*, pages 113–14 for a use of this method) it cannot satisfy us today. What the psalmist meant is perfectly clear, and no responsible use of the Bible can make it mean what the author could not possibly have intended.

Should we, then, omit the verses, as recommended in 1916 by the Archbishop's commission? If we do, we shall be losers. We shall lose a passage which, by its very offensiveness, claims our attention, and which then begins to interrogate us. We live in a world in which victorious armies commit atrocities against their defeated enemies. Do people who have seen their menfolk executed and their women and children sexually abused have no feelings of revenge? Can we be sure that, if we had been on the receiving end of such abuse, we would not also long for revenge?

In my opinion, we should use Psalm 137 in the following way. We should pray the whole of it as members of a fragmented and cruel humanity that actually carries out such deeds and also longs for revenge. This will remind us of what is so nobly stated in Psalm 130:3–4. We shall have no cause to boast of human achievements.

We shall look to God alone as the one who can heal a broken and fragmented human race.

GUIDELINES

Our psalms in week 1 affirmed that the experience of God in prayer and worship helps us to be certain about God's faithfulness, and sustains us when all the cards seem to be stacked in favour of the unjust and powerful. What happens, however, when we do not have the certainty that prayer and worship bring? Several of this week's psalms express such a hopelessness, especially Psalms 88 and 137, and they, together with 109 and 129, take refuge in vindictive thoughts against enemies, or meditate in satisfaction upon Israel's victories over her enemies.

It is good that these psalms are in the Bible, for many believers experience periods, short or long, when prayer and worship result more in frustration than in communion with God. It can help them to know that they are not the first or only ones to feel like this.

What can we say positively? First, we must never forget that spiritual depression is a religious experience. We would not feel as we did if we did not care for the things of God. Secondly, we may find Psalm 130 useful, as we acknowledge our weakness before God and marvel that the One who knows our faults is also the One who accepts and affirms us. Thirdly, and this is a primary duty for those who are *not* experiencing difficulties in prayer and worship, we must pray these psalms on behalf of a broken and shattered humanity, many of whose members see no hope and can only think of vengeance. We must ask God to use our hope (which is God's gift) to transform their despair.

9–15 DECEMBER

1 A new song *Read Psalm 96*

In this final week of meditation upon selected psalms, the choice has been made of psalms which bring together some of the themes from weeks 1 and 2, but which put them in the context of a celebration of the manifestation of God's redeeming love.

Psalm 96 touches on the themes of other gods, the joy of entering the sanctuary, and the sea (depths) joining in the praise of God. In Psalm 82 the gods appointed to oversee the nations are condemned to death because they have not upheld justice for the poor and defenceless. Psalm 96 goes further and says that other gods are merely idols—the work of human hands. But this is not an expression of Israelite religious imperialism, an exultation that *Israel's* God has triumphed. As we saw when reading Psalm 129, what matters to the Old Testament is not the triumph of a *national* God, but the triumph of a *universal* justice longed for by all those within the nations who are upright in heart (Psalm 94:15). Thus, this Psalm is not merely an Israelite celebration. The whole earth is invited (v. 1) and the good news is to go out to all nations (vv. 3, 7).

If the writer of Psalms 42 and 43 is sad at exclusion from the sanctuary, Psalm 96 looks forward to a time when all people will be invited to worship there. If Psalm 130 is prayed from the depths of a sea which represents chaos and danger, Psalm 96 portrays the sea as joining in the praise to God, together with fields and forests.

There is a very ancient Christian tradition that the words 'the Lord has reigned from the tree' originally followed the words 'The Lord is King' in verse 10. This addition was never part of the psalm, but it is an illuminating comment upon the psalm from a Christian viewpoint. All the language about kingship and victory has ultimately to be understood in terms of the one whose kingdom was based upon the power of suffering love, whose throne was a cross, and whose victory was a life laid down for others.

2 The Lord is God *Read Psalm 100*

Psalm 100 concentrates upon the theme announced in Psalm 96, that all nations should join in worshipping God in the sanctuary. The opening verse calls upon the earth, meaning all the peoples on earth, to shout in acclamation to God. The peoples are to enter God's presence singing songs of joy, because his rule of justice and peace has been established.

Verse 3 needs particular attention. It begins with a call to 'know that the Lord, he (alone) is God'. The REB 'acknowledge' for the Hebrew 'know' perhaps puts the emphasis in the wrong place: it suggests the outward and verbal expression of a fact, whereas the Hebrew is referring to an inner conviction about the lordship of God which is not only an intellectual conviction, but one born of trust in God. The Prayer Book version 'be ye sure that the Lord he is God' gets something of this.

In the second part of verse 3 there are two possible interpretations based upon two traditions within the Hebrew text. The written text has 'it is *he* who made us and not we (ourselves)'. The hymn 'All people that on earth do dwell', which is a metrical version of Psalm 100, follows this interpretation in the words 'without our aid he did us make'. However, there is a Hebrew tradition that the word 'not' should be read as 'to him', and this yields the rendering '*he* it is who made us, and we are his'. This adds the new thought that all the peoples of the world belong to God, because he is their maker.

Verse 4 speaks of entering the sanctuary. The temple in Jerusalem was not a large cathedral-like building, but a series of open-air courtyards in the centre of which stood a structure housing the holy of holies. The psalm, then, does not envisage the entry into a building, but of crowds thronging together in great open spaces, proclaiming the steadfast love of God.

But how can we sing this song in a broken and fragmented world? We can only do so if we cherish it as a vision of what could be here on earth if the nations knew that the Lord alone is God, and if we are encouraged by that vision to work and pray for a better world.

3 Hope for the poor and weak *Read Psalm 113*

This is a particularly appropriate psalm for the period leading up to Christmas because it contains one of the most sublime expressions in the Old Testament of how God is both exalted above the heavens and yet concerned for the most vulnerable people on earth. These sentiments are expressed in verses 5–6, whose Hebrew is clear, but difficult to put into English. The Hebrew is literally: 'Who is like the Lord our God who makes himself high to dwell; who makes himself low to see; in heaven and on earth.' The words 'in heaven and on earth' are not governed by the verb 'to see' (thus the Prayer Book's 'yet humbleth himself to behold the things that are in heaven and earth' is incorrect). Rather, 'in heaven' complements the phrase 'makes himself high to dwell' and 'on earth' complements 'makes himself low to see'. The REB is therefore misleading; and it should be added that the REB 'deigns' is not contained or implied in the Hebrew.

When read in the light of Christmas, the psalm takes on a new dimension. In its own terms, it describes God's active compassion for the poor and vulnerable in terms of placing them among princes. No doubt there are many poor people who would like to join the ranks of the wealthy and privileged. Again, readers (whether men or women) who are sensitive to women's issues will read verse 9 in the context of a culture in which childlessness was a disgrace and the bearing of many children a blessing, without wanting to apply these values mechanically to our own society.

In fact, the incarnation of God in Jesus Christ expresses God's exaltedness and participation in the things of earth in an unexpected way. In Jesus, God rescues the poor not by giving them a place with princes, but by coming among them and by redefining what is meant by rank and power. He rescues women by affirming them as they are, rather than in terms of cultural expectations. A Christian reading of this psalm is a sharp reminder that in applying values to our world, we need to have that mind that we find in Christ Jesus (see Philippians 2:5, and the rest of that passage to v. 11).

4 Thanksgiving for deliverance *Read Psalm 116*

This psalm is the counterpart to psalms such as Psalm 88. As opposed to the unrelieved pessimism of that psalm, Psalm 116 is full of light and joy. The psalmist has experienced troubles similar to those that we find in other laments. Thus, he found himself so close to death that it was as though the underworld (*Sheol*) was dragging him down (v. 3). Again, the psalmist had so come to despair about the goodness or loyalty of other people that he had proclaimed 'how faithless are all my fellow creatures' (v. 11).

However, while other psalms dwell on the troubles facing the psalmist, this psalm concentrates upon the faithfulness and compassion of the God who had delivered him.

Yet we need to qualify this statement in an important way, and then take the results back to the more pessimistic psalms that we have read. The cynic might say of the psalmist's words in this psalm, 'He would say that, wouldn't he? After all, he had got what he wanted.' But there is more to this psalm than a merely mechanical relationship between the psalmist getting what he wants (i.e. deliverance from his troubles) and his fulsome praise of God. God is not a gadget whose purpose is to help the psalmist get whatever he wants. Through his troubles and his deliverance the psalmist has drawn close to God. He wants to describe his relationship to God in terms of being God's slave (v. 16), and he does not mean by this an abject surrender of his personality, but a dedication of his gifts to God's service (cf. vv. 12–14). If he commends God's goodness to others (cf. vv. 14, 18) it will be in terms of the joy of knowing in a deep and intimate way that God is gracious (v. 7), not the recommendation of God as an automatic rescuer in time of trouble.

This brings us back to the more pessimistic psalms, for they are precisely the proof that God is *not* an automatic device for rescuing the needy. We do not know why God can apparently deliver some people from their troubles, but not others; we do not know why we find *both* Psalms 88 and 116 in the Psalter. But we do have both psalms, and we have to say, paradoxically, that 88 is as much an expression of faith as 116. Perhaps it is a *greater* expression of faith, given that the psalmist's prayers received no apparent answer. Neither did the prayer of Jesus in Gethsemane, that the cup should pass from him (Mark 14:36).

5 Restored fortunes *Read Psalm 126*

If Psalm 116 can be seen as a counterpart to Psalm 88, then 126 can be viewed similarly in regard to 137. In the latter psalm, even if the psalmist has returned from exile in Babylon, Jerusalem is apparently still in ruins and there is no joy in the psalm, only resentment against enemies. In Psalm 126 the tide has turned and this event has produced joy and laughter. Yet the psalmist may be facing new difficulties (v. 4), but facing them in the assurance that, in God's designs, troubles do not last for ever, and that joy follows weeping.

Verse 1 contains two problems of translation. The rendering 'when the Lord turned again the captivity of Zion' familiar from the Prayer Book and Authorized Version, takes a particular Hebrew word to mean 'captivity'. But it can also be translated as 'turning', yielding the phrase 'when the Lord turned the turning (i.e. fortunes) of Zion' as in the REB. Although this latter translation removes from the verse a direct reference to the return from exile in Babylon, it is still this event that is most probably in mind. The second matter is whether to take a particular word to mean 'to dream' or 'to be healthy'. The former is certainly the more poetic, being a Hebrew equivalent of our phrase 'it was too good to be true'.

Verse 4 possibly sets the psalm in a time of trouble after the return from exile, or expresses the anxiety of a community for whom the hopes aroused by the return from exile had not been fulfilled. It is even possible that the psalm was occasioned by a succession of poor harvests.

The Negeb, the dry south of the land, normally receives only a low rainfall, yet there can be years when the rain is sufficiently copious for dry river beds to become abundant streams. Again, in spite of the hard toil involved in preparing soil for the sowing of seed, the harvest will be a time of joy. However, this should not be thought of as an automatic process from which God is excluded. The joy of harvest is a reminder of the joy experienced by the believing community when God upholds his promises in furtherance of his plan to bless all peoples (v. 2b).

6 True confidence Read Psalm 146

This psalm is the ultimate expression of confidence in God, who alone can be trusted to establish justice on earth. Previous psalms, such as 58 and 94, have had harsh things to say about those in power who rule unjustly. Here, the same sentiments are expressed, but more generally, and in the context of reliance on God alone.

The psalmist advises that we should not trust any human ruler. All such people and their plans come to nothing, a point that will not be lost on a reader in the twentieth century who has seen the great empires established by leaders such as Hitler and Stalin come to nothing. Against the transitory power of mortal human rulers, the psalmist emphasizes how God maintains faithfulness and justice (vv. 6–7). Five times in verses 7–10 the psalmist puts 'the Lord' in an emphatic position as the one who deals graciously with prisoners, the blind, the bowed down, the righteous, and the fatherless and the widow (this is slightly obscured in the REB).

However, we are entitled to ask whether this psalm is realistic. Can God do things for those who are unjustly imprisoned, or who are blind or bowed down, etc. without human agency; and if human agency is involved, is there not the danger that we shall have to rely on human plans and organizers, against the advice of verses 3–4? And if God is going to bypass all human agency, is he not like the sort of executive who delegates nothing to subordinates?

If we read the psalm in this way we shall ignore all that we have read in previous psalms about the (usually failed) obligation of rulers and ordinary people to act humanely. We therefore need to take Psalm 146 to imply that we should not trust those princes and mortals who exercise their power while disregarding God, and that we need to strive for a world in which human exercise of power is truly in accordance with God's will. And we can do this best of all by never forgetting that only Jesus Christ lived a life fully in accord with the will of God.

GUIDELINES

This week's psalms place us in the company of a celebrating and rejoicing throng; a company that looks forward in eager anticipation to the triumph of God's purposes. This will be a triumph welcomed by all peoples and by the powers of nature, including fields and forests (natural features that are under threat of their existence in today's world).

Where did the psalmists get their confidence from? Not from a contemplation of the world around them. The psalms of weeks 1 and 2 have shown how little there was to choose between their world and ours when it comes to brutality, dishonesty and corruption. Their confidence came from a special knowledge of

God that was contained in Israel's traditions, celebrated in prayer and worship, and refined by trial and adversity. We also have access to this resource, as well as to that further disclosure of God in the life, teaching, death and resurrection of Jesus. He fulfils many of the hopes expressed in this week's psalms, and it is no accident that the Psalms were constantly in his mind, especially on the cross.

Further reading

R. Davidson, *The Courage to Doubt: Exploring an Old Testament Theme*, SCM Press, 1983

J.W. Rogerson and J.W. McKay, *Psalms: Cambridge Bible Commentary*, Cambridge University Press, 1977

Christmas and New Year readings

The readings are based on John 1:1–18, which is one of the Gospel passages appointed for Christmas Day. They can be used with any version of the Bible.

16–22 DECEMBER

John 1:1–10, 14–18

1   The Word *Read John 1:1–2*

'Thus says the Lord'… 'Then God said, "Let there be light."' We are used to the idea (as expressed for example in the Psalms and in the creation stories of Genesis 1–3) that God is not a remote God, too far away to communicate with this world. God made the world through divine command, and God's ways have been made known to humankind by the words of the prophets and in the words of the Bible.

'Word' is one of the key means by which God reaches out and becomes intimately related to this world. But 'word', as in 'speaking', is not the only meaning of 'the Word' here in John's Gospel. For the Jews God's 'word' did indeed indicate an intimate link between God and the world; in the Stoic philosophy prevalent at the time, '*Logos*' (the Greek word for 'word' used here) signified the divine spirit which dwelt within and ordered the world.

John here is meditating on the significance of Jesus Christ (possibly using a traditional hymn). As God's Word Jesus Christ is the manifestation of God's very self. Over this Christmas period we shall be looking at this from many different perspectives by means of an extended meditation on John 1:1–18. You should read through the whole passage each day before looking at the notes on particular verses, so as to think through with John the meaning of the incarnation. That way, we too might come and worship.

2 Creation *Read John 1:3, 10*

'All things came into being through him.' This is worth comparing to Colossians 1:15–20, where Christ is described as the one in or by whom God both created and redeemed all things. The identification of Jesus Christ the agent of creation with Jesus Christ the agent of redemption means that we must never think of the created world as evil, as opposed to a good spiritual realm; or think that the laws of God's kingdom are somehow not for this world (like, for example, saying that women are equal with men in the final redemption but are to be subordinate in this world).

'Lo, within a manger lies, he who built the starry skies': Many of our Christmas carols speak of this role of Jesus Christ in creation. The early Christians, in their attempts to understand who Jesus was and how they could interpret his significance, associated him with the Wisdom of God. They drew attention to passages such as Proverbs 8:22–31: 'then I was beside him like a master worker...' to illustrate Wisdom's involvement in creation.

'Wisdom', or '*Sophia*' in Greek, is a feminine symbol and concept, unlike 'Logos' (see the previous notes) which is masculine. Looking at the idea of Wisdom in Jewish and Christian scripture and philosophy can help us realize that, although Jesus was a male human being, neither maleness nor indeed masculinity are part of the revelation of God's essential self.

How might we take to ourselves the meaning of Jesus Christ as agent of creation this Christmas?

- *First, we might remember that Jesus came to redeem us from what has gone wrong in the world, not from the world as such.*

- *Secondly, we should condemn most strongly the way in which Christmas can be used as an excuse for economic exploitation and greed.*

- *Thirdly, we can enjoy most heartily the celebration of the good gifts which God has given us in this world.*

3 Life *Read John 1:4*

'I am the resurrection and the life' said Jesus to Martha, whose brother Lazarus had died (John 11:25). 'The thief comes only to steal and kill and destroy; I come that they may have life, and have it abundantly' (John 10:10).

Life is not only about creation and joy, it is also seen most clearly in the context of death, and that which destroys life. In the birth of the baby Jesus we are reminded of both death and life. It is not only that all over the world many newborn babies die, and indeed mothers die in childbirth, it is also that to be born inevitably means that death will come to us one day—we are all mortal. And Jesus was no exception. Simeon warned Mary that 'a sword will pierce your own soul too', as he looked to what lay ahead for Jesus (Luke 2:35).

A new birth is always a death of something for the new mother; Jesus' birth represented the death of so much for so many. Simeon again said: 'This child is destined for the falling and the rising of many in Israel.'

To speak of death here is not to give death the last word, but rather to assert that 'in him was life'—a life which is triumphant over the darkness.

4 Light *Read John 1:4–9*

At a Carols by Candlelight service the congregation often starts in darkness, then a single candle is lit to symbolize Christ, the light of the world. Gradually the whole church fills with light as the light of Christ overcomes the surrounding darkness; more and more candles are lit to symbolize the enlightening of all people.

The contrast of light and darkness is deeply ingrained in Christian tradition, and one place where it is constantly found is in the Gospel of John. These are symbols with which we must be very careful because they can so easily be misused. As human beings we are all complex mixtures of good and bad, of light and darkness. When an individual or a group identifies themselves with 'the children of light' rather than the 'children of darkness' they tend to forget their own 'dark side', and to project on to the others everything that is wrong and evil. This has happened so often in Christian history, for example in the 'demonization' of Jews by Christians or of women by men. Jesus Christ is the light of the world, but Christians must remember that they and their religion need the help of that light just as much as anyone else does.

But, careful though we must be, we cannot ignore these symbols and the reality which stands behind them. Imperfect though our judgment and motives must be, it is imperative that we care about right and wrong, about justice and injustice, about the promotion of love and peace. There is indeed darkness in this world. Insofar as we truly follow Christ, and are enlightened by him, our lives will expose it and bring light and life into that darkness.

5 Witness *Read John 1:6–9, 14–18*

Surely there is no Christian who has not asked themselves at some time, 'Why is it that I believe what I do? How can I be sure my faith has integrity? Is God really as I have learned God to be through my Christian faith?'

We do not have any *direct* access to knowledge of God, except possibly through certain kinds of mystical experiences. One of the primary ways in which we come to know what is true about God is through witness or testimony. This witness is cumulative. Here John speaks of the witness of John the Baptist. In John 8:18 Jesus testifies on his own behalf and also points to the testimony of the Father, the works that Jesus does through the Father (see John 10:38). We can add to this the testimony of the Bible, the witness of Christians down the centuries, and indeed of our own friends.

Karl Barth, the great twentieth-century Swiss theologian, speaks of witness as being like when you come across a group of people looking up into the sky and *pointing beyond themselves* to a reality which no one can totally grasp but which is nonetheless real.

The Greek word for 'witness' is '*marturia*', from which our word 'martyr' comes. For many of the early Christians, and indeed for many Christians in various parts of the world today, witness to Jesus and his ways means martyrdom, torture and death. Their suffering points beyond themselves to the God who is acknowledged and honoured, just as Jesus' crucifixion glorified God (cf. John 17:1–5).

Even amid the rejoicing of Christmas we are reminded that the three wise men brought not only gold to bear witness to a king, and frankincense to bear witness to deity, but also myrrh to foreshadow the witness of Jesus' suffering.

6 John the Baptist *Read John 1:6–8, 15, 17*

You may find it helpful to read verses 19–37 of this chapter. Here, John is a voice, a pointer. Not the Messiah, not the light, but the one who came 'baptizing with water for this reason, that he might be revealed to Israel' (v. 31). There is even more about John in the other Gospels. He was the greatest of the prophets of the old order, but he pointed to someone yet greater, on whom the Spirit would descend and *remain*; and to something yet greater—not just the baptism of the repentance but the baptism of the Holy Spirit.

It is interesting how John's words and actions push us in the very direction he has declared—to talk about the person and work of Christ rather than the person and work of John himself. John and Jesus both preached repentance in the face of the coming kingdom of God. The difference between them, in this passage, is the role they play within that kingdom: John merely announces; but Jesus' relationship with the Holy Spirit gives him a more pivotal role. In Jesus, God indeed comes to dwell with God's people, through the permanent presence of the Holy Spirit—first in Jesus the Messiah (the Anointed One), and secondly in those whom Jesus has empowered to baptize with the Spirit.

At Christmas we remember 'Immanuel'—God with us. This is the unique role and status which we, with John the Baptist in this passage, assign to Jesus and to no other human being in the same way.

GUIDELINES

See how from far upon the eastern road
The star-led wizards haste with odours sweet!
O run, prevent them with thy humble ode,

And lay it lowly at his blessed feet;
Have thou the honour first thy Lord to greet,
  And join thy voice unto the angel quire,
From out his secret altar touched with hallowed fire.

John Milton, from 'Ode on the Morning of Christ's Nativity'

23–29 DECEMBER   JOHN 1:10–18

1   The world did not know him *Read John 1:10–11*

This theological truth is powerfully symbolized for us at Christmas as we tell the story of how there was 'no room at the inn'. Poor innkeeper! He was only protecting his other guests, and he has been given the villain's line in every nativity pageant since. But that is because this is *symbolic*. It is symbolic of every individual's refusal to admit the love and demands of God; it is symbolic of the fact that the Jews of Jesus' own day did not recognize their salvation when it came to them (v. 11); it is symbolic of the resistance of the whole world to honour or give thanks to God the Creator (see Romans 1:20–21).

It is very important that we read verse 11 alongside verse 10. There has been a tendency in Christian tradition to blame the Jews for their rejection of Jesus, without seeing how much we also have been guilty. A superficial acknowledgement of Christianity is not good enough. When Christians refuse to acknowledge Jesus by spurning his way of love, his concern for the outcast, peace, courageous integrity, and putting the kingdom of God above material wealth and ambition, they are as guilty of 'not knowing him' as were the Jews of his day. They as good as ignore or reject Christ.

In Luke 4:24 we read that those who 'know' Jesus best are those least likely to know and understand him most truly: 'no prophet is accepted in the prophet's home town'. We should heed this warning deeply. The philosopher Bertrand Russell, in an essay explaining why he was an atheist, wrote that he greatly admired the teachings of Jesus but that the Church had betrayed them ever since. Many would recognize the truth of that viewpoint from their own experience.

2 Children of God *Read John 1:12–13*

We have already looked at Jesus, the one who baptizes with the Holy Spirit. (Notice that this is not a reference to some dramatic, ecstatic experience, but to being brought into a new and intimate relationship with God.) Here we are offered a different image for the same experience. (It is impossible to speak of these things except in images; language about God must always use analogy— 'like' this, without being exactly the same as this.) This new image is that of *birth*; the new relationship we enter into with God through Christ is compared with being born.

In Jesus' conversation with Nicodemus in John 3:1–10 this idea is developed further. Here, the main point is that it is an act of God's will, comparable to the decision of a human being to have a child, which brings us into relationship with God. Perhaps this is a particularly apt image to think about at Christmas, as it not only leads us to think of the human birth of Jesus, but also reminds us that all that happened in Jesus was by the will of God. We must never separate God from Jesus, so that we think of God as a cold judge and Jesus as the compassionate one who secures our forgiveness. *We are made children of God by the will of God.*

But no image is perfect, and this one has been used to denigrate the human processes of birth, counting the spiritual ministrations of (often celibate) priests in symbolizing the new birth in baptism as worth more in the eyes of God than the very earthy and fleshly processes of physical birth, from which a woman even had to be 'cleansed'.

There is no need, however, to take it this way. Talk of blood and flesh here is followed immediately by verse 14: 'And the Word became *flesh*'. The whole point of the Christmas story is that God did not shrink from human flesh (did not abhor it, as the *Te Deum* says) but was born as a real 'flesh and blood' baby.

3   'And the Word became flesh and lived among us' *Read John 1:14*

In the early days of Israelite history the Ark of God, which symbolized the presence of God, moved around in a tent with the people in their wanderings. The word used for 'lived' here is the word for living in a tent; God in Christ has come to dwell among us, to be God's presence with us wherever we go, to live under the same conditions as us.

We looked at the 'Word' last week, God's eternal 'connected-ness' with this world. Today we think of that Word becoming flesh, becoming a little baby.

The kind of Christmas Day sermon which likens the miracle of God's becoming a human being to communicate with us, to our becoming, say, a hamster to communicate with our pets, has simply missed the point. What the birth of Jesus, interpreted as the incarnation (the 'enfleshment') of God, teaches us is that being human is not incompatible with being God. We have learned in Jesus something new about what it means to be God.

We have also learned something new about what it means to be human. The early theologians of the Church spoke of the 'divinization' which is possible in Christ. Because God, in Christ, has become what we are, then what we are is healed and saved, and we can become what he is.

Because 'being flesh' is not incompatible with 'being God', and because God has indeed 'become flesh' in Jesus Christ, then we know also that the human condition, with all its pain and suffering as well as its joy, is never Godforsaken. At Christmas we celebrate the particular pains and joys in which God was present in human childbirth.

4   Glory *Read John 1:14; Revelation 1:12–18*

God's glory is the outward, visible quality of God's splendour and holiness. We have *seen* God's glory in Jesus Christ.

Revelation 1 describes a vision of the risen Christ seen by John (probably not the same John who wrote the Gospel). Christ's glory here is conveyed in terms of splendid clothes, white hair, flaming eyes, a voice like many waters, a two-edged sword and the power of resurrection over death.

By contrast the glory which 'we have seen' in John 1 refers to a very earthly life—with resurrection at the end, it is true, but with crucifixion and death before that. Jesus lived a fully earthly life, sharing all the discomforts and the temptations of the human condition, and showing in human love the love of God for the poor, the sick and the outcast. Jesus' human life began in an animals' feeding box in overcrowded Bethlehem.

In Jesus Christ we learn the truth of the paradox in both descriptions of God's glory. God is appropriately spoken of in terms of power and splendour—indeed Jesus speaks in John 17:5 of the glory he had in God's presence 'before the world existed'. But God's power and splendour are most clearly revealed in God's own emptying of self in Jesus:

> *'Thou who wast rich beyond all splendour*
> *All for love's sake becamest poor.'*

5 A Father's only Son *Read John 1:14, 18*

'Take your son, your only son… whom you love…' So spoke God to Abraham (Genesis 22:2). We cannot read these words in John without thinking back to Abraham's being ready to sacrifice his only son, and thinking forward to Jesus' death on the cross.

In today's reading the emphasis is not primarily on the sacrifice, but on the special quality of the relationship between Jesus and God the Father. Christians know God as 'the God and Father of our Lord Jesus Christ'. This, amongst other things, is expressed in our doctrine of the Trinity, and was the object of much controversy in the early Church. Was Jesus to be described as being 'of like substance' to God or 'of the same substance as God'? The latter was declared to be orthodox belief. This unique relationship which Jesus had to God led Christians to describe him as 'begotten, not created'; in other words, the way in which God is Father of Jesus is different from the way in which God is Father of us.

These questions are still debated and important, however obscure they sometimes seem to be, because what is at stake is the status of the revelation of God in Christ Jesus. John's Gospel falls on that side of the debate which wants to emphasize the uniqueness and superiority of Jesus' relationship as the only Son of the Father, and therefore the uniqueness and reliability of Jesus' revelation of God: 'Not that anyone has seen the Father except the one who is from God; he has seen the Father,' (John 6:46).

Jesus speaks and acts as he has learned from the Father and in obedience to the Father: 'I speak these things as the Father instructed me… for I always do what is pleasing to him' (John 8:28–29). Being the Son is not only to do with some mysterious 'sharing the very substance of God', it is also about living a *life* in obedience to the Father.

So let us think back to Abraham—'your only son, whom you love'. When John speaks of Jesus as God's only Son, he speaks of the deep love within God, of the preciousness of the Son to the Father. In this relationship love is declared to be part of the very essence of God: not just the way God *feels towards* the created world, but the way God *actually is*.

6 Grace *Read John 1:14–18*

Grace is a word which reflects the very essence of the gospel. Interestingly here it is shown both in its discontinuity and its continuity with God's already existing covenant with the Jewish people.

'The Law indeed was given through Moses; grace and truth came through Jesus Christ.' Is it an 'and' or a 'but' which is implied in the middle of that verse? Does the 'new' covenant *contradict* the 'old' or *build* upon it? Christians have often preferred the former, but notice how close 'grace and truth' is to the 'mercy and steadfast love' which characterize the description of God's covenant in the Psalms, God's 'abundant' love, which comes 'from his fullness… grace upon grace'.

The contrast between 'Law' and 'grace' has often been presented as a contrast between Judaism and Christianity. Jesus posed it as two ways of understanding God within Judaism, as he preached and lived out the good news of God's acceptance of all, including sinners and outcasts. Today we see the contrast most clearly as a contrast between two ways of preaching and living out Christianity.
law v grace

There is a kind of Christianity which is more concerned for the moral backbone of the world (not to mention the Church!), and is more afraid of seeming to condone sin than of offending against God's grace and mercy. Those who are caught in this trap are not free to live the gospel. There are no doubt reasons of psychology and personal biography which affect how much grace we can accept for ourselves, and how much we can show to others. This should not, however, make us hopeless or fatalistic about growing in grace. The whole point about grace is that it is not dependant on us, but comes to us from the God who is 'greater than our hearts' (1 John 3:20).

GUIDELINES

Behold the great Creator makes
   Himself a house of clay,
A robe of virgin-flesh he takes
   Which he will wear for aye.

Hark, hark, the wise eternal Word
   Like a weak infant cries:
In form of servant is the Lord,
   And God in cradle lies.

This wonder struck the world amazed,
   It shook the starry frame;
Squadrons of spirits stood and gazed,
   Then down in troops they came.

Glad shepherds ran to view this sight;
   A quire of angels sings;
And eastern sages with delight
   Adore this King of kings.

Join them all hearts that are not stone,
   And all our voices prove,
To celebrate this holy one,
   The God of peace and love.

Thomas Pestel, 'Psalm for Christmas Day'

1   Truth *Read John 1:14, 16; 18:33–38*

'What is truth?' asks Pilate of Jesus. 'Factual accuracy', we might at first answer, but that would fall well short of the mark. Jesus speaks of something much more deep and complicated than that; he speaks of 'belonging to the truth'. What does he mean?

Jesus connects this with listening to his voice: 'Everyone who belongs to the truth listens to my voice.' Truth is an important concept in John's Gospel. The 'Word made flesh' is full of truth, and truth comes to enlighten us all through him. Indeed Jesus describes himself as 'the truth' (John 14:6). So the meaning of truth and of belonging to the truth has first and foremost to do with the truth about God as it is known in Christ.

We cannot separate this out as if it were 'religious truth', unconnected with the sometimes very pressing questions of truth which arise for us in our everyday lives. 'I am the way, the truth and the life': truth is integrally related to life and the way it is lived. This gives us a clue about how to approach matters of truth in our daily lives when 'factual accuracy' is neither remotely accessible, nor by any means the most significant factor.

Take the example of Jesus' trial. Here he is, involved in a desperately complex life situation, with accusations flying all over from different parties: complex mixtures of truth, lies and misunderstandings. How like our own lives this is, from comparatively trivial family squabbles, to the breakdown in marriage or workplace relationships.

The first thing to notice about Jesus is that he has a high view of truth: he identifies it with the deepest form of understanding and commitment to God. Secondly, Jesus has a realistic notion of people's capacity to understand truth: he explains what he can to Pilate, but without banging his head against a brick wall. Thirdly, he has a realistic understanding of the way people use and distort 'truth' to their own ends: 'Do you ask this on your own, or did others tell you about me?' Truth is not just a commodity there for the taking: people's right to the truth depends on how they are going to use it. Finally, although Jesus doesn't waste his words in fruitless argument, his vision is not deflected from the truth which he knows, and his actions are guided by his vision. This is integrity, which is an important part of truth.

2   Revelation of God *Read John 1:18*

In one sense there is nothing more to add here, other than to refer back to everything which we have thought about over the last two weeks. 'No one has ever seen God', but what we have seen is Jesus. Or rather, what others saw and testified to was Jesus, and we have their testimony, written here for us in John's Gospel.

We have considered the ways in which Jesus is 'close to the Father's heart', and how that puts him in a unique position to reveal God to us. But there is another place in the Bible where the words 'no one has ever seen God' are used. It is in 1 John 4:12, which continues, 'if we love one another, God lives in us, and his love is perfected in us'. This connects the revelation of God to the world through Christ with the revelation of God to the world through the love which the followers of Christ have for one another.

The text is realistic: it does say 'if' not 'when'! However it might be appropriate, after all the celebrations of Christmas, when we have remembered the gift of God to us in Jesus, to consider that 'since God loved us so much, we ought to love one another' (1 John 4:11). This way the revelation of God's love in Jesus continues in our lives in the new year.

Guidelines © BRF 1996

Published by
The Bible Reading Fellowship
Peter's Way, Sandy Lane West,
Oxford, OX4 5HG
ISBN 0 7459 3257 6

Distributed in Australia by:
Albatross Books Pty Ltd, PO Box 320,
Sutherland, NSW 2232, Australia

Distributed in New Zealand by:
Scripture Union Wholesale, PO Box 760,
Wellington

Distributed in South Africa by:
Struik Book Distributors, PO Box 193,
Maitland 7405

Distributed inthe USA by:
The Bible Reading Fellowship, PO Box M,
Winter Park, Florida 32790

Publications distributed to more than 60
countries

Acknowledgments

Revised Standard Version of the Bible
copyright © 1946, 1952, 1971 by the
Division of Christian Education of the
National Council of the Churches of Christ in
the USA.

New Revised Standard Version of the Bible,
copyright © 1989 by the Division of
Christian Education of the National Council
of the Churches of Christ in the USA.

Revised English Bible © 1989 by permission
of Oxford and Cambridge University Presses.

Cover photograph: Richard Fisher

Printed in Denmark

SUBSCRIPTIONS

❑ I would like to give a gift subscription (please complete both name and address sections below)

❑ I would like to take out a subscription myself (complete name and address details only once)

❑ Please send me details of Life Membership Subscriptions

This completed coupon should be sent with appropriate payment to BRF. Alternatively, please write to us quoting your name, address, the subscription you would like for either yourself or a friend (with their name and address), the start date and credit card number, expiry date and signature if paying by credit card.

Gift subscription name _____

Gift subscription address _____

_____

_____ Postcode _____

Please send to the above, beginning with the Sep 1996/Jan 1997 issue (delete as appropriate): (please tick box)

		UK	SURFACE	AIR MAIL
GUIDELINES		❑ £9.00	❑ £10.00	❑ £12.50
NEW DAYLIGHT		❑ £9.00	❑ £10.00	❑ £12.50
NEW DAYLIGHT LARGE PRINT		❑ £15.00	❑ £15.00	❑ £17.50

Please complete the payment details below and send your coupon, with appropriate payment to: **The Bible Reading Fellowship, Peter's Way, Sandy Lane West, Oxford OX4 5HG**

Your name _____

Your address _____

_____

_____ Postcode _____

Total enclosed £ _____ (cheques should be made payable to 'BRF')

Payment by cheque ❑ postal order ❑ Visa ❑ Mastercard ❑ Switch ❑

Card number: ☐☐☐☐☐ ☐☐☐☐☐ ☐☐☐☐☐ ☐☐☐☐☐

Expiry date of card: ☐☐☐☐ Issue number (Switch): ☐☐☐☐

Signature (essential if paying by credit/Switch card) _____

NB: BRF notes are also available from your local Christian bookshop.

GL0396   The Bible Reading Fellowship is a Registered Charity

BIBLE READING RESOURCES PACK

Not all churches celebrate Bible Sunday on the second Sunday in Advent (8 December 1996), so from September 1996 we are producing a Bible Reading Resources Pack which will be available throughout the year. The Resource Pack for 1996/97 will include a poster, sample editions of the notes, magazine articles, ideas for promoting Bible reading in your church and much more. Unless you specify the month in which you would like the pack sent, we will send it immediately on receipt of your order. We greatly appreciate your donations towards the cost of producing the pack (without them we would not be able to make the pack available) and we welcome your comments about the contents of the pack and your ideas for future ones.

This coupon should be sent to:

The Bible Reading Fellowship
Peter's Way
Sandy Lane West
Oxford OX4 5HG

Name _____

Address _____

_____

_____ Postcode _____

Please send me _____ Bible Reading Resources Pack(s)

Please send the pack now/ in_____ (month).

I enclose a donation for £_____ towards the cost of the pack.

The Bible Reading Fellowship is a Registered Charity

BRF PUBLICATIONS ORDER FORM

Please ensure that you complete and send off both sides of this order form.

Please send me the following book(s):

	Quantity	Price	Total
A Gallery of Reflections: the Nativity of Christ	_____	£11.99	_____
Sunday by Sunday (Year 1)	_____	£11.99	_____
The Jesus Prayer	_____	£3.50	_____
Prophets & Poets	_____	£8.99	_____
Sowers & Reapers	_____	£9.99	_____
The Matthew Passion	_____	£5.99	_____
Day by Day for Windows	_____	£25.00	_____
Struck By Jesus Daily Notes	_____	£2.50	_____
Out of This World Daily Notes	_____	£2.99	_____
Getting to Grips with God Daily Notes	_____	£2.99	_____

POSTAGE AND PACKING CHARGES			
order value	UK	Europe	Surface	Air Mail
£6.00 & under	£1.25	£2.25	£2.25	£3.50
£6.01–£14.99	£3.00	£3.50	£4.50	£6.50
£15.00–£29.99	£4.00	£5.50	£7.50	£11.00
£30.00 & over	free	prices on request		

Total cost of books £ _____

Postage and packing £ _____

TOTAL £ _____

(see over for payment details)

All prices are correct at time of going to press, are subject to the prevailing rate of VAT and may be subject to change without prior warning.

NB: All BRF titles are also available from your local Christian bookshop.

GL0396   The Bible Reading Fellowship is a Registered Charity

PAYMENT DETAILS

Please complete the payment details below and send with appropriate payment and completed order form to:

The Bible Reading Fellowship,
Peter's Way,
Sandy Lane West,
Oxford OX4 5HG

Name _____

Address _____

_____

_____ Postcode _____

Total enclosed £ _____ (cheques should be made payable to 'BRF')

Payment by cheque ❑ postal order ❑ Visa ❑ Mastercard ❑ Switch ❑

Card number: ▯▯▯▯ ▯▯▯▯ ▯▯▯▯ ▯▯▯▯

Expiry date of card: ▯▯▯▯ Issue number (Switch): ▯▯▯▯

Signature (essential if paying by credit/Switch card) _____

Alternatively you may wish to order books using the BRF telephone order hotline: 01865 748227

The Bible Reading Fellowship is a Registered Charity